THE WEIRDEST HISTORY REPORT EVER

ANT PELLICANO

Copyright © 2026 by Anthony Michael Pellicano

All rights reserved.

No part of this publication may be reproduced, distributed, or transmitted in any form or by any means, including photocopying, recording, or other electronic or mechanical methods, without the prior written permission of the publisher, except as permitted by U.S. copyright law. For permission requests, contact Anthony Pellicano.

This writer acknowledges the difficulty of verifying certain facts in historical accounts and has made every effort to ensure accuracy. But, due to secondhand accounts and limited hard evidence, some details may be subject to interpretation.

Edited by Alissa Depietro

Book Cover by Anthony Michael Pellicano

Authors Note:

The stories in this book are shortened versions of real events with time travel added.

If a particular story interests you, this author encourages you to learn more.

"A day without learning is a day wasted. There is so much to learn and so little time to learn it" – Albert Einstein

Table of Contents

Extras

From Classroom to Time Capsule

One Friday morning in April at New Port Richey High School, a school assignment is going to change three kids' lives forever.

The sound of chatter and shuffling papers filled the room as Mr. Pellicano scanned the faces before him. His classroom was a mix of anxious freshmen, restless students, and those dreaming of the weekend ahead. The clock on the wall ticked loudly, counting down the final minutes of a typical Friday afternoon.

Mr. Pellicano cleared his throat, his voice cutting through the noise. “Alright, settle down, everyone. I’ve got a special assignment for you.”

The class slowly quieted, curious now.

“This isn’t going to be your average history report,” he said, a slight smile tugging at the corners of his mouth. “This project will count for half your grade. So, I want you to take it seriously, but at the same time, I want it to be fun and interesting. Your task: find the weirdest, most unbelievable story in American history. On Monday, you will be presenting your report to the class.”

A ripple of excitement spread through the room. “Weirdest story?” someone muttered.

“Exactly,” Mr. Pellicano continued. “It could be a strange invention, a bizarre event, a forgotten battle, anything that makes you say, ‘Wait, that actually happened?’ You’ll work in groups of three.”

He began calling out names from his list, pairing students up. The class hushed as each group formed.

“Rose and Lilly, you’re together.”

Rose sat up straighter, her dark eyes bright with anticipation. Lilly, sitting next to her, smiled warmly and gave a small nod.

“And Hayden,” Mr. Pellicano said, “you’ll join them.”

Hayden’s head snapped up, surprised and unsure. He had been quietly trying to stay under the radar, juggling his ‘D’ average and trying not to attract attention.

Rose looked at Hayden with a curious smile. “Hey,” she said softly, “welcome to the group.”

Lilly nodded. “Yeah, it’s nice to have you.”

Hayden shuffled his backpack straps, still looking uncertain. “Uh, thanks. I’ll do my best.”

The bell finally rang, and the noise in the room erupted again. Students grabbed their things, talking excitedly about the new project. Rose, Lilly, and Hayden gathered their backpacks and started toward the door.

Outside, the school hallway was packed with students. Lockers slammed, and voices echoed off the tiled walls.

Rose glanced at Hayden. “So, what kind of weird stories do you think we should look for?”

Hayden shrugged. “I dunno. Weird stuff usually means trouble, right?”

Lilly smiled thoughtfully. “Sometimes the strangest stories have the most interesting truths behind them.”

Rose chimed in. "It has to be really weird. Remember, Mr. Pellicano used to work at the Neon Oasis Casino, so I'm sure he's seen some weird stuff."

They walked in silence for a moment until Rose stopped near the science room, glancing around to make sure no one was watching.

Rose reached into her backpack and pulled out a strange-looking device. It was about the size of a small cellphone, covered in buttons, blinking lights, and wires running in every direction.

Lilly's eyes widened. "Whoa. What is that?"

Hayden leaned closer, eyebrows raised. "Looks like something out of a sci-fi movie."

Rose's voice dropped to a whisper. "This is a Chronojumper. It's my time machine."

Hayden blinked. "No way. You're kidding. How did you find that in New Port Richey, Florida?"

Rose shook her head, a proud smile spreading across her face. "I built it myself, over the past year, in my garage."

Lilly stared at it, her excitement barely contained. "You mean... we could actually travel back in time?"

Rose nodded. “Exactly. We can visit the events we’re studying, see history with our own eyes.”

“Before I agree to travel through time with you, I have to ask. How exactly does this thing work?” Lilly asked.

Rose turns the chronojumper toward Lilly and Hayden. “It’s powered by a cell phone battery and run by an AI that follows my every command.”

“Your AI?” Lily asked.

Rose smiled. “It’s called the Advanced Learning Intelligence for Supporting Spacetime Adventures or A.L.I.S.S.A. for short.”

A voice came from the chronojumper. “Hello, where would you like to go today?”

Hayden laughed nervously, a mix of disbelief and excitement. “This is crazy. But... I’m in. Let’s do it!”

The three of them made their way to Rose’s house, talking quietly about what stories they might uncover.

Rose explained, “I’m glad we got this project because I get to finally test this thing. What better way than to use it than to find the most unbelievable story in American history and experience it firsthand?"

Lilly added, "I've always loved history, but I don't want to be a test dummy."

"It's perfectly safe I tested it with an apple. I sent it forward in time one hour and it came out mostly intact." Rose replied.

"Mostly?" Lilly aid with a confused look.

Rose smiled, "I'm joking. It worked perfectly."

Hayden still looked a little skeptical but intrigued. "I just hope we don't mess up history like bring the dinosaurs back."

"Dinosaurs?" Lilly questioned.

"I saw it in a movie once."

Rose smiled nervously. "I trained ALISSA to search the internet in the present day and remove all references to us in the past. We'll still have to be careful not to change too much."

"Oh, great," Hayden replied.

Rose led them into a cluttered garage with posters of historic figures lining the walls. Tools and wires were scattered on the tables. The time machine sat in the center, humming softly, waiting.

Hayden looked over the console, eyes wide. “So, where do we go first?”

Lilly reached into her backpack and pulled out a purple notebook. “I wrote down some interesting things Mr. Pellicano said happened in history. Let’s use this as a guide and see where history takes us.”

Hayden gasped. “A lot of those places look pretty sketchy. Is this going to be dangerous?”

Rose smiled. “We’ll be safe... I think.”

Hayden swallowed hard, suddenly nervous. “This feels real now.”

Lilly squeezed his arm. “We’ll stick together.”

Rose grabbed the chronojumper. “Ready?”

They all nodded, holding hands for a second, hearts pounding.

Their adventure had begun.

The Wild West Was Real

The garage was alive with the soft hum of the chronojumper as Rose, Lilly, and Hayden gathered around the glowing screen.

“Okay, team,” Rose said, tapping her tablet, “we’re heading to one of the most legendary places in American history, Tombstone, Arizona Territory, October 23, 1881.”

Lilly’s eyes sparkled with excitement. “The real Tombstone home of Wyatt Earp, Doc Holliday, and the infamous O.K. Corral shootout. This was a turning point in the Wild West.”

Rose nodded eagerly. “This was the Wild West at its wildest: lawmen, outlaws, revenge, and justice all tangled together.”

Hayden scratched his head. “I know the movie makes it look like a big Hollywood showdown, but was it really that dramatic?”

Lilly smiled. “It was dramatic, but also way more complicated. Let’s go see for ourselves.”

Rose grabbed the chronojumper “ALISSA, show us the life of Wyatt Earp.”

ALISSA responded, “Three... two... one...” A large blue circular portal opened up in the middle of the garage, and the teens held hands as they walked through.

Just as soon as they entered the portal, they exited, and when the world snapped back into focus, the trio stood on a dusty street under a blazing sun. The air was thick with the scent of dry earth, horse sweat, and pine tar.

Before them lay Tombstone, a bustling frontier mining town surrounded by jagged desert hills, wooden sidewalks creaked beneath feet; wagon wheels clattered; horses neighed and stamped.

Lilly scanned the scene. “Tombstone was barely four years old but already full of opportunity and trouble. Miners, ranchers, gamblers, and gunslingers all fought to make their mark.”

Hayden squinted at the buildings. “It looks like a movie set... but people lived here for real?”

Rose nodded. “And the stakes were life or death. There was gold, greed, and a constant battle between order and chaos.”

Rose pointed across the street. “There, you can see the ‘Cowboys’, a loosely organized gang involved in cattle rustling, gambling, and sometimes murder.”

Hayden whispered, “So they were basically the bad guys?”

“Sort of,” Rose said. “They weren’t just outlaws, though they had a complicated relationship with the townsfolk and each other. But they certainly opposed the Earps.”

Lilly added, “Wyatt Earp was one of Tombstone’s lawmen, along with his brothers Virgil and Morgan. They wanted to bring order to the chaos.”

The teens watched as Wyatt Earp, tall and serious, spoke quietly with Virgil and Morgan near a busy saloon.

“Wyatt’s reputation as a lawman was growing,” Lilly said. “He had experience from other frontier towns, and he wasn’t afraid to enforce the law.”

Rose added, “But the Cowboys ran many of the town’s illegal businesses. They saw the Earps as a threat.”

Hayden asked, “Did the Earps and Cowboys get along at all?”

“Not really,” Lilly replied. “There were constant tensions. Fistfights, threats, even shootings.”

Rose, Hayden, and Lilly set up camp just outside of town, and over the next few days, the teens witnessed several arguments between the cowboys and people of Tombstone.

One afternoon, near a gambling hall, a Cowboys gang member, Ike Clanton, loudly accused the Earps of trying to shut down his illegal activities.

Wyatt calmly told him to follow the law, but Ike insulted Wyatt in return.

Lilly explained, “Ike Clanton was one of the main troublemakers, always looking for a fight.”

Rose nodded. “The Earps tried to keep peace, but they weren’t afraid to confront the Cowboys when they crossed the line.”

Another day, the teens saw Doc Holliday arrive, a pale, sharp-eyed gambler and Wyatt’s close friend who suffered from tuberculosis.

“Doc was deadly with a gun,” Lilly whispered. “But also loyal to Wyatt.”

Over the next couple of days, the teens heard rumors that the Cowboys planned to intimidate or attack the Earps.

The Earps warned the Cowboys to leave town or face arrest.

On October 25, 1881, things came to a head.

The Earps and Doc received reports that Ike Clanton and several Cowboys were armed and causing trouble near the corral.

Wyatt, Virgil, and Morgan rode out with Doc to confront them.

Rose, Hayden, and Lilly watched eagerly, hearts pounding, as the two groups faced each other near the dusty O.K. Corral.

Wyatt called out for the Cowboys to disarm.

Ike Clanton refused, shouting threats.

There was a stretch of tense silence. Then gunfire erupted quick, fierce, and deadly.

Back behind a nearby building, Rose, Lilly, and Hayden ducked. The sounds of bullets and shouting filled the air in a cloud of smoke.

When the smoke cleared, three Cowboys lay dead, and the Earps and Doc stood covered in the blood of those who tried to kill them, unharmed.

Lilly sighed. “That shootout was brief but deadly and just the climax of months of build-up.”

Rose said, “The O.K. Corral fight turned Wyatt Earp into a legend, but the real story is much messier. This was only the beginning of a violent struggle for control of the West.”

After the fight, the trio followed the Earps and Doc to the Bird Cage Theatre, a dimly lit gambling hall and saloon where many of Tombstone’s deals and secrets unfolded.

Inside, Wyatt leaned on the bar, exhausted but alert.

Lilly said softly, “Wyatt wasn’t just a gunslinger; he was also a gambler, a businessman, and a family man.”

Rose added, “He believed in law and order, but he had to fight for it.”

Hayden asked, “But why didn’t the Cowboys just back down?”

Lilly explained, “Remember, they were making a lot of money from their illegal activities. They weren’t going to give that up without a fight.”

Rose nodded, "The Earps threatened their power and profits. The conflict escalated into ambushes, revenge attacks, and legal battles"

Hayden blinked in disbelief. "So, this wasn't just one fight, it was years of violence?"

Lilly nodded. "Exactly. Tombstone was a wild, dangerous place where justice was personal and deadly."

Rose said, "And Doc Holliday was by Wyatt's side, battling his own illness but fiercely loyal."

Lilly nodded grimly. "This wasn't the end. For the Earps, it was the beginning of something worse."

The chronojumper opened a portal behind them, but Rose held up a hand. "Let's not leave yet. We need to see what came after."

They fast-forwarded just a few months. It was now March 19th, 1881, and Tombstone had grown darker. The once-busy streets were quieter. The townspeople walked quickly, eyes wary.

"Virgil Earp was ambushed just weeks after the O.K. Corral," Rose explained as they passed a boarding house. "He was shot in the back with a shotgun, crippled for life."

“By the Cowboys?” Hayden asked.

“Almost certainly,” Lilly said. “But no one was convicted.”

The teens slipped into the Oriental Saloon, where Wyatt sat alone at a corner table, a cup of coffee in front of him. His eyes were sunken and heavy. The lawman who once stood tall now looked like a man consumed by grief.

“Wyatt later admitted never showed much emotion,” Rose whispered. “But inside, he was burning.”

Lilly added, “And then, in March 1882, they killed his brother Morgan.”

Hayden froze. “They what?”

“Shot through a window while Morgan was playing pool,” Rose said. “Killed instantly.”

The next day Morgan’s coffin was being loaded onto a train, headed home to California. Wyatt, dressed in black, watched with hollow eyes.

"That was the final straw," Lilly said. "Wyatt had tried to do things by the book. Arrests, trials, warnings. But Tombstone's justice system had failed."

"So, he gave up on the law," Rose said. "And picked up a shotgun."

The chronojumper opened a portal. It was April 5th, 1882, and the trio now stood outside the mining camp of Iron Springs.

Wyatt Earp rode into view on a chestnut horse, his long black coat flapping behind him. Beside him: Doc Holliday, his brother Warren Earp, and a handful of trusted deputies.

"This was the Vendetta Ride," Rose said. "Wyatt hunted down the men responsible for Morgan's murder and Virgil's ambush."

They watched as Wyatt dismounted silently. Gunfire erupted moments later. Cowboys caught in their tents, surprised and outgunned.

The teens flinched as Wyatt burst through a canvas tent, shotgun raised. One of the Cowboys tried to run. A single shot dropped him.

"That was Curly Bill Brocius," Lilly said, breathless. "The Cowboys' leader. Wyatt killed him right here. In the middle of a gunfight with bullets whizzing past him."

“He just walked through the gunfire?” Hayden whispered.

Rose nodded. “He was a man possessed. Some said he couldn’t be killed.”

Over the next ten days, the Earp posse crisscrossed the Arizona desert, tracking down Cowboy leaders one by one. They found them in canyons, ranch houses, and saloons.

Justice wasn’t coming from a courtroom anymore; it came from the barrel of Wyatt’s gun.

“The townspeople were divided,” Lilly said. “Some thought Wyatt was a hero. Others saw him as a vigilante.”

Rose added, “Eventually, the Governor ordered him to stop. But by then, most of the Cowboys were dead, in hiding, or scattered.”

Later, the teens overheard Wyatt Earp and Doc sitting around a campfire.

Wyatt’s voice was steady but weary. “The West isn’t a place for the faint-hearted. Sometimes you've got to take the law into your own hands.”

Doc Holliday, coughing but sharp-eyed, added, “It’s a brutal world, but loyalty and courage are what matter most.”

Hayden whispered, “It’s easy to think of them as heroes or villains, but they were real people with tough choices.”

Lilly said, “And their story shaped the myth of the Wild West.”

Rose smiled, “We have to tell this story, honestly, with all its grit and complexity.”

The chronojumper beeped gently.

ALISSA said, “Time to go.” Before opening a portal in front of them.

They walked through the portal to Los Angeles on January 2nd, 1907.

Wyatt Earp, older, grayer, but still strong, sat on a porch with his second wife, Josie. A newspaperman interviewed him nearby.

“He never went to jail for what he did,” Lilly said. “He outlived almost everyone from Tombstone.”

Rose whispered, “And before he died in 1929, Hollywood started making Westerns. Directors went to Wyatt for advice.”

Hayden shook his head. “So, the movies True Grit, Pale Rider, Tombstone, all of them started with him?”

“Pretty much,” Rose said. “He helped shape his own legend as well as the legend of the wild west itself.”

“But the real Wyatt?” Lilly added. “He was tougher, more complicated. A man who tried to follow the law... until it failed him.”

“This is the end of Wyatts story.” ALISSA said as the chronojumper opened a portal home.

Back in the garage, the chronojumper powered down.

Lilly opened her notebook. “Okay. For the report, we’re not just talking about the O.K. Corral. We’re talking about everything. What drove Wyatt Earp from lawman to vigilante?”

Lilly grinned. “The history is deeper than the movie. Real lives, real struggles.”

Rose nodded. “Perfect for our report.”

Hayden laughed, “I just hope our teacher likes history with more dust and drama.”

The chronojumper sat humming on the table. The journey wasn't over

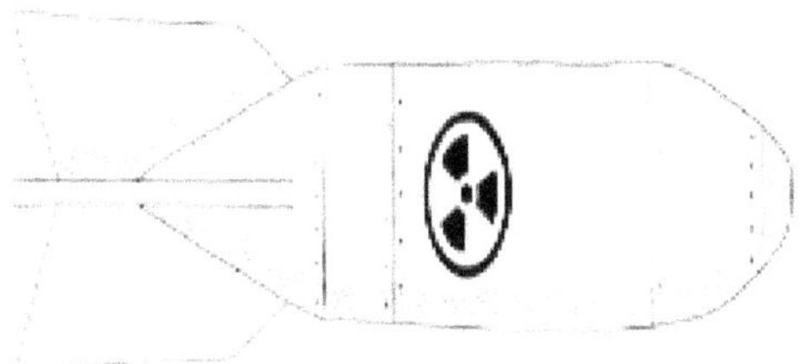

The Day America Nearly Nuked Itself

The garage was unusually quiet, except for the gentle hum of the chronojumper warming up. Rose tapped on her tablet, scrolling through Lilly's notebook.

"Okay," she said, looking up, "this next one's not about war heroes or spies. It's about the U.S. government almost nuking itself. Twice."

Hayden blinked. "Wait. Like... they dropped nukes? On purpose?"

Lilly leaned in, eyebrows raised. "Technically? No. Accidentally? Yes."

Rose grinned. "Next stop: Goldsboro, North Carolina. January 23rd, 1961. ALISSA show us the end of Operation Chrome dome."

“As you wish.” ALISSA responded, “Opening a portal now.”

The teens emerged on a quiet stretch of farmland under a cloudy dawn sky. A thin mist hugged the fields. Everything seemed peaceful.

Until a distant roar shattered the silence.

Overhead, a B-52 Stratofortress screamed through the clouds, clearly in distress.

"That plane’s falling apart!" Hayden shouted, shielding his eyes.

Lilly nodded. "It's got a fuel leak and structural failure. And it's carrying two Mark 39 thermonuclear bombs."

"This was during the height of the Cold War. Nukes were being flown around constantly. The idea was to have them ready to launch at any time, just in case America was attacked by the Soviet Union."

"So, we had armed bombs in the sky, 24/7?" Hayden asked.

"Pretty much," Lilly said. "It was called Operation Chrome Dome. Planes took off with nukes and stayed in the air for hours just to be ready."

But this one was in trouble. Severe turbulence had ruptured a fuel line, causing the right wing to break off.

The plane cracked apart in the air. Flaming debris spiraled down, and then two massive objects fell free, plummeting toward the earth.

BOOM.

A deafening thud shook the ground. Dirt erupted into the sky.

“That did not sound good, but how bad could it really be?” Hayden commented.

"Both of those were fully armed," Rose muttered, watching the chaos unfold.

“So that bad. Forget I said anything,” Hayden said in shock.

"We came seconds away from losing the East Coast." Rose added.

The teens ran to a nearby hilltop, where emergency crews were beginning to arrive. In the middle of a massive crater lay a partially buried nuclear bomb.

"The parachute deployed," Lilly said. "Which slowed it down. But that’s not the only reason this isn’t a nuclear wasteland right now."

Rose pointed to a clipboard one of the Air Force officers carried. "Four of the five safety switches failed. Only one switch stopped that bomb from detonating."

Hayden swallowed hard. "So… we were one switch away from vaporizing half the state?"

"Yup," Rose replied. "And not just North Carolina. This baby had a yield of about 4 megatons. It would've destroyed everything from D.C. to Raleigh. That's almost 300 miles or 5,000 football fields!"

Lilly added, "One of the switches failed due to the same stress forces that would happen during an actual nuclear launch. The safety systems were basically a coin toss."

The teens watched as military crews surrounded the area, digging through the field with bulldozers and Geiger counters, also known as radiation detectors.

"The second bomb sank deep into the mud," Lilly said. "They never recovered all of it. Part of the nuclear core is still buried here."

Hayden backed away from the hole. "And we're just... standing on it?"

Rose nodded. "It's sealed. Mostly. But yeah, welcome to America's glowing backyard."

A specialist nearby said quietly to another, "We got the arm/safe switch intact. But I swear, one more jolt, and this thing would've been toast."

Rose gathered the group around a chalkboard inside a temporary Air Force tent.

"So, here's what happened," she began. "This B-52 was flying a long-range patrol loaded with two live nukes. But the right wing had a known design flaw that made it vulnerable during refueling."

"They were trying to meet up with a tanker when the plane started leaking fuel and lost control," Lilly continued. "Eventually, the wing just snapped off."

"The bombs were ejected during the breakup," Rose added. "One of them deployed its parachute. The other slammed straight into the ground."

"Because they were armed," Lilly said, "it went through nearly the entire detonation sequence. One switch, one single 28-volt switch, saved millions of lives."

Hayden raised his hand. "That switch deserves a medal."

"It kinda got one," Rose said. "After this, engineers completely overhauled the way nukes were designed and carried."

“All of the safety measures on both nukes failed except one.” Lilly said, “The crazy part is the single safety switch that worked was different on each bomb.”

Rose explained the broader picture.

"But the more you fly with nukes," Rose added, "the more chances something can go wrong."

"And it did," Lilly continued. "There were over 30 documented 'Broken Arrow' incidents. This one just nearly ended in an apocalypse."

“What’s a broken arrow?” Hayden asked.

Rose chimed in, “That’s when the government loses a nuke.”

Hayden's face turned white, “30! I hope someone gets fired for this. I get in trouble when I lose my homework, and this is way worse.”

“History shows this event is over,” ALISSA said as the chronojumper opened a portal home.

Back in the garage, the chronojumper powered down with a soft hum. Everyone looked a little rattled.

"So," Hayden said, sitting down, "we almost nuked North Carolina. Twice."

Rose nodded. "And it wasn't the last time something like this happened."

"There was even a 1968 case where a B-52 crashed off Greenland with four nukes on board," Lilly added. "It melted part of the ice shelf."

Hayden groaned. "Why is this not in our textbooks?"

Rose clicked her pen. "Because it's easier to hide near-catastrophes than to explain them."

Lilly looked thoughtful. "But every one of these close calls pushed nuclear safety forward. This incident directly led to improved failsafes and stricter procedures."

"So... hooray for almost blowing up?" Hayden asked.

They laughed nervously.

Rose wrote the new title in her report:

"One Switch from Oblivion: The 1961 Goldsboro Broken Arrow Incident."

The chronojumper hummed again.

"Let’s pick something a little less radioactive next time," Hayden said.

Rose smirked. "No promises."

History's Bravest Horse

The garage was quiet, except for the clink of Hayden dropping a half-eaten candy bar onto the floor.

"Alright," he said, wiping his hands on his hoodie, "we've done cowboys and nuclear bombs. What's next? Jetpack ninjas?"

Rose rolled her eyes and adjusted the dials on the chronojumper. "Actually," she said with a grin, "we're going to Korea. 1953. To meet a Marine... who's a horse."

Hayden blinked. "Excuse me?"

Lilly was already flipping through her notebook. "Sergeant Reckless," she said with reverence. "War horse of the 5th Marines during the Korean War."

"She carried ammo," Rose explained, "through open fire, uphill, alone. Again, and again. They promoted her to Staff Sergeant. And yes, she was a horse."

"Now that is a history report," Hayden said as the chronojumper began to hum.

Rose grabbed the chronojumper. “ALISSA, show us the life of Sergeant Reckless.”

A portal opened up for the teens once again.

It was March 13th, 1953 - Outskirts of Outpost Vegas, Korea

The air was frigid. Smoke curled over bombed-out hills. The teens crouched behind a pile of spent artillery casings as Marines scrambled to reload a 75mm recoilless rifle.

Then, from behind the hill, came the steady clop-clop-clop of hooves.

"There she is," Lilly whispered, pointing.

A chestnut Mongolian mare trotted into view, her back loaded with six heavy artillery shells in canvas slings. A Marine gave her a gentle pat as she passed.

"That's Reckless," Rose said. "Originally named 'Flame,' a racehorse bought for 250 bucks from a South Korean boy whose family needed money. The Marines trained her to deliver ammo and evacuate wounded."

"You're telling me they brought a racehorse to a gunfight?" Hayden asked.

"And she crushed it," Lilly said. "She memorized the routes. She ducked incoming fire. She crossed minefields alone."

Artillery thundered around them. Reckless didn't flinch.

They watched her climb the steep slope toward the front line. Bullets cracked overhead. Shrapnel hissed through the air.

"During the Battle for Outpost Vegas," Rose said, "she made 51 solo trips in one day. She hauled over 9,000 pounds of ammo."

"And she was wounded twice," Lilly added. "Still kept going."

They followed her to the top of the hill, where Marines fired round after round at Korean positions in the distance.

One of the Marines turned to another. "Give her a Hershey bar when she gets back. And a beer."

Hayden did a double take. "They gave her beer?"

"She loved it," Rose grinned. "Beer, scrambled eggs, Coca-Cola, peanut butter sandwiches. Classic Marine."

Later That Evening at a Marine Camp behind the lines, the teens watched as a corpsman patched up a minor shrapnel graze on the side of Reckless.

"She saved lives," Lilly whispered. "Without her, the gunners would've had to carry the shells themselves under fire. She gave them time, cover, and hope."

"The Marines treated her like one of their own," Rose said. "She slept in tents with them. Walked into mess halls. They even gave her a rank."

Hayden blinked. "So, she outranked privates?"

"By the end of the war," Lilly said proudly, "she was a Staff Sergeant. Officially promoted. With full honors. No soldier with a rank below her was allowed to ride her. Also, if she outranked you and you had food or beer that she wanted, it was considered an order to give it to her."

Rose grabbed the chronojumper out of her pocket. "This is getting too dangerous. Let's regroup at my house."

The garage was dim except for the glowing chronojumper screen. Hayden stretched and yawned. "So, what happened to Reckless after all that? Did she retire to some fancy farm?"

Rose smiled as ALISSA spoke through the chronojumper. "I'll show you."

A portal opened to June 20th, 1955, in Camp Pendleton, California.

The teens appeared near a peaceful paddock fenced off with wooden rails. Reckless, now older but still proud, grazed quietly, her chestnut coat gleaming in the sunlight.

"After the war, she lived here," Lilly said, running her fingers along the fence. "Camp Pendleton was her home base."

A Marine approached, carrying a brush and a bucket. He smiled warmly at the mare and began grooming her.

"She wasn't just a warhorse," Rose said. "She became a symbol of courage and loyalty. Marines loved her like family."

Hayden watched as Reckless flicked her ears, content and calm. "Did she ever go back to racing?"

Lilly shook her head. "Nope. She was done with that. Her job was done. The Secretary of the Marines ordered nothing to be put on her back heavier than her blanket."

Hayden pulled out his cell phone and searched for images of Reckless. The screen showed videos of a parade in Washington, D.C. Crowds lined the streets, cheering. Marines marched past in dress blues. Reckless, draped in her medals, walked proudly at the front.

"She even attended the Marine Corps birthday ball in 1954," Rose added. "The only horse ever invited."

Hayden laughed. "Imagine showing up to a fancy party and being the only animal there."

The teens now stood in a quieter paddock. Reckless, older, and a little slower, rested under a shady tree. A few Marines gathered nearby, telling stories about her heroic runs.

"She passed away peacefully in 1968," Lilly said softly. "But her story didn't end there."

The chronojumper opened a portal to modern day at the National Museum of the Marine Corps, the teens found themselves inside the gleaming museum in Quantico, Virginia. They stood before a towering bronze statue of Sergeant Reckless, her proud head held high.

"This is her legacy," Rose said. "Remembered for bravery, perseverance, and loyalty."

A plaque read:

"Sergeant Reckless, the War Horse of the Marines, who carried more than 9,000 pounds of ammunition through battle under fire, twice wounded, and loved by all who served with her."

Hayden looked up at the statue. "Not bad for a horse, huh?"

Lilly grinned. "She showed everyone that sometimes heroes come with four hooves and a whole lot of heart."

Hayden cracked a smile. "Should we salute?"

Lilly rolled her eyes. "If you want to."

Rose laughed. "No saluting the statue, Hayden."

Rose closed the notebook. "That's the story we're bringing back. 'Sergeant Reckless: The War Horse Who Fought With Marines.'"

“You survived your first war,” ALISSA said as the chronojumper opened a portal home.

Back in the garage, the chronojumper powered down. The teens sat in silence.

"So," Hayden said, "we just met a literal war horse who outran machine guns and drank beer with Marines."

"That’s Sergeant Reckless to you," Rose corrected.

Lilly nodded. "Report title: Four Hooves, Fifty Missions."

"Let’s hope Mr. Pellicano agrees," Rose said. "Now, who's up for visiting the Boston Tea Party... or maybe the day the CIA tried to spy on cats?"

Hayden raised his hand. "Do either involve more animals?"

"Possibly," Rose smirked.

The chronojumper began to hum again.

How Chocolate Fought Communism

The garage buzzed with quiet electricity as Rose picked up the chronojumper dial.

"Want to see how America fought communism with chocolate?" Rose said with a grin.

Hayden jumped up. "Is that even a question? Heck yeah!"

"ALISSA show us the Berlin Airlift," Rose asked, eyes gleaming. "This one is about courage, cold war tension, and... candy parachutes."

"As you wish." ALISSA responded, "Opening a portal now."

Hayden grinned, “Candy parachutes? Now that sounds promising.”

Lilly flipped open her notebook. “June 24, 1948. The Soviets just blocked all road, rail, and canal routes into West Berlin. The city was trapped.”

Hayden groaned. “Trapped? Like a cage?”

Rose nodded. “Exactly. West Berlin was surrounded by Soviet-controlled East Germany. The Soviets wanted to force the Allies out.”

The teens walked through the portal to the rain-slick streets of a ruined Berlin on January 24, 1949.

Lilly pointed at the distant border, “Months ago the Soviets closed all the supply routes. No food, no coal, no medicine. West Berlin’s two million residents were cut off overnight.”

A nearby Berliner woman pulled her child closer, whispering nervously.

Hayden looked around wide-eyed. “How did the people survive?”

Rose said, "At first, the Allies thought the Soviets might give up, but it was clear Berlin needed help. That's when the U.S. and British came up with a crazy plan fly everything in by air."

The teens stood near a muddy trench by the side of a shattered building, listening to the distant roar of aircraft overhead.

Hayden wiped rain from his face. "So… why are the Soviets trying to starve out the city? I mean, just to make a point, right?"

Lilly folded her arms. "It's more than that. The Soviets wanted to spread communism, control governments, economies, and even people's lives."

Rose nodded seriously. "Exactly. The Soviet Union believed in a totalitarian system, where the state controls everything and individual freedoms don't matter."

Hayden frowned, "But isn't communism supposed to be about fairness? Like sharing everything equally?"

Lilly shook her head gently. "That's the theory. But in practice, especially under Soviet leader Joseph Stalin, it became oppressive. People lost their rights, those who opposed were subdued, and fear ruled."

Rose added, "The blockade was a way to pressure the West to abandon West Berlin and let it fall under Soviet control. They wanted to expand their influence over Europe."

Hayden looked uneasy. “So, this isn’t just about a city or supplies. It’s about a whole way of life?”

Lilly’s voice was quiet but firm. “Yes, and the Allies believed that if communism spread unchecked, it would threaten freedom everywhere.”

Rose’s eyes scanned the horizon. “That’s why the Berlin Airlift was so important. It was more than just planes dropping food; it was a stand against totalitarianism.”

Hayden sighed. “No wonder people risked their lives flying those missions. It was a battle for freedom.”

Rose smiled softly. “History isn’t just about dates and battles. It’s about ideas and the choices people make.”

Lilly tapped her notebook. “This conversation will make our report stronger, explaining why the airlift mattered politically and personally.”

Hayden grinned. “And reminding us that standing up for freedom takes guts.”

The teens walked to a roaring airfield at Rhein-Main, Germany. C-47 Skytrains and giant C-54 Skymasters lined up, engines roaring.

"Operation Vittles was launched. This was the code name for the airlift," Rose explained.

Lilly added, "They started with 32 flights a day. By November, planes landed every 30 seconds!" She tapped her notes eagerly.

Hayden whistled, "Every 30 seconds? That's insane!"

A pilot walking by overheard them.

"You think this was easy?" he said, laughing. "Try landing with fog, snow, and under enemy eyes."

Rose, Lilly, and Hayden fell silent for a moment and found themselves watching coal sacks and flour barrels unloaded under gray skies.

Lilly explained, "Berlin needed about 4,500 tons of supplies daily to survive winter. That meant nonstop flights 24/7."

Rose nodded grimly. "Temperatures plunged below freezing. Crews worked fast but cautiously."

Hayden shivered. “That must have been terrifying. One mistake, and everything could go wrong.”

As dusk settled, a friendly pilot approached the teens.

“That’s Lt. Gail Halvorsen,” Rose said softly. “He started dropping candy to children, using little parachutes made from handkerchiefs.”

Halvorsen smiled warmly. “Kids called me ‘Uncle Wiggly Wings.’ It started with just a few chocolates but turned into Operation Little Vittles.”

Hayden laughed. “So even in war, candy made people smile?”

Lilly nodded. “Yes. The candy drops became a symbol of hope in a desperate time.”

Suddenly, a Soviet MiG jet buzzed low over the airport, searchlights scanning.

Rose whispered, “Soviets tried to intimidate Allied pilots, but never fired. They feared full-scale war.”

Lilly added, “But there were accidents. Over 100 airmen died from crashes, fog, and mechanical failures.”

Hayden swallowed. “The stakes were real.”

Lilly pointed out, “It wasn’t just the U.S. The British Royal Air Force, plus Australia, Canada, France, New Zealand, and South Africa helped.”

Hayden grinned, “A real team effort.”

The chronojumper flickered again and it was May 12, 1949. Suddenly, the tense skies lifted as Allied planes flew freely.

“On May 12, 1949, the Soviets lifted the blockade,” Rose announced.

Lilly smiled, “But the airlift didn’t stop immediately—they kept flying until September 30 to build stockpiles.”

Hayden looked impressed. “Planning ahead.”

The teens walked through a sunlit Berlin park, watching children play with parachute candy.

Lilly whispered, “Berliners saw Allied pilots as heroes.”

A Berliner woman smiled, holding a chocolate wrapper. “Thanks to them, we lived through the coldest winter.”

Hayden's eyes shone. "Sometimes something as small as flying candy can bring people together in the hardest times."

"I hope you have seen enough for your report." ALISSA said as the chronojumper opened a portal home.

"Yes, I believe we have. Thank you, ALISSA." Rose replied as she and the others walked through the portal.

Back in the garage, the teens exchanged thoughtful looks.

Rose jotted down: Report Title: "The Berlin Airlift: How Planes and Parachutes Saved a City."

Lilly added, "The airlift showed logistics, courage, and kindness can win even the toughest battles."

Hayden grinned, "And always pack candy."

They laughed as the chronojumper hummed to life, ready for the next adventure.

World War Tree

The garage hummed with tension as Rose picked up the chronojumper.

"Okay," she said, looking up, "You want to see a tree that almost started World War Three?"

Hayden gulped. "Something about a tree starting a war? I'm not sure my brain can handle this."

Lilly clicked her pen. "On August 18th, 1976, a simple poplar tree in the Korean Demilitarized zone (DMZ) nearly sparked World War III."

Rose looked at the chronojumper, "ALISSA take us there."

"As you wish." ALISSA responded, "Opening a portal now."

Rose, Lilly, and Hayden walked through the portal and into a crisp morning scene in the Joint Security Area (JSA), a small settlement located near the village of Panmunjom, South Korea, where North Korea and South Korea (plus the United Nations Command) can meet face-to-face. North and South Korean guards stood a few meters apart like sentinels. The tension in the air was almost physical.

Lilly murmured, "This is the infamous poplar tree that blocked the view between the two countries' checkpoints."

Rose nodded. "United Nations Command decided to trim it back. Nothing too crazy, just strategic visibility."

The teens watched as U.S. Army Captain Arthur Bonifas and South Korean Captain Kim led a small team of Korean Service Corps workers, axes in hand.

Hayden squinted. "That tree looks harmless enough."

Suddenly, 15–35 North Korean soldiers surrounded them.

One Korean officer simply known as "The Bulldog" barked, "Kim Il-sung planted that tree! You will not touch it!"

The workers paused. Bonifas turned back. Defiance in his eyes.

Then chaos erupted. North Koreans attacked with axes and clubs. Bonifas and First Lieutenant Mark Barrett were struck down, each killed in minutes, and others were wounded.

Hayden whispered, "That escalated fast."

Lilly added, "A routine pruning turned into the Axe Murder incident, serious stuff."

The news raced back to Washington. President Ford and Secretary Kissinger made crisis calls. DEFCON 3 status loomed for U.S. forces in Korea. At one-point, nuclear war was on the table.

Rose tapped the notebook. "They debated bombing or psy-ops... but decided on a super-sized tree-trimming instead."

Lilly nodded. "They planned Operation Paul Bunyan: a forced tree removal with overwhelming show of force plus helicopters, jets, and Marines. The largest display of controlled aggression since the Korean War."

"Taking you to Operation Paul Bunyan, August 21st, 1976," ALISSA said as the chronojumper opened a portal in front of the teens.

Rose, Hayden, and Lilly walked through the portal, moving forward in time but staying in the DMZ. While staying a safe distance, the teens hid and watched the US and South Korean forces mobilize to take down a simple tree.

The US and South Korea managed to bring together:

23 vehicles.

Two 30-man security platoons escorting chainsaw teams.

64 Korean Special Forces with rifles and grenade launchers.

Cobra helicopters, utility choppers, F-4 Phantoms.

Nuclear-capable B-52s circling overhead.

USS Midway task force offshore.

12,000-plus troops on alert.

Lilly whispered, “It was the most expensive tree-trimming in history.”

Hayden couldn't help laughing, “Of course it was. Only America would turn landscaping into a military campaign.”

It was 7AM and the Americans walked up to the tree with roaring chainsaws in hand.

The poplar tree shuddered. North Korean guards stared, wildly outnumbered and completely overwhelmed.

Security platoons showed their clubs; helicopters hummed above. Tension crackled louder than the saws.

Within minutes, the tree thudded to the ground. A twenty-foot stump remained left deliberately.

Not a shot fired.

North Korea backed down, accepting responsibility and expressing "regret." Captain Bonifas and Lt. Barrett were promoted following their passing. Camp Liberty Bell was renamed Camp Bonifas.

"Looks like you survived another close call" ALISSA said as the chronojumper opened a portal home.

Back in the garage, the chronojumper powered down. But instead of heading to their laptops, Rose led the others outside. "There's someone we need to talk to," she said.

At a quiet neighborhood park, an elderly man sat beneath a maple tree. He wore a weathered ballcap marked "DMZ Security Battalion," and leaning beside him was a dark, polished stick.

"Mr. Livsey?" Rose asked softly.

The man looked up. His eyes were sharp but kind. "Yes?"

"We're doing a report on Operation Paul Bunyan," Lilly said. "We read that you carried the swagger stick carved from the poplar tree."

He tapped it lightly on the ground. "This one right here. A reminder of the day we nearly lost everything over a tree."

Hayden sat beside him. "Weren't you scared?"

He smiled faintly. "Terrified. But also… determined. We weren't going to let two of our own be murdered without standing tall."

Rose studied the stick. "It's beautiful."

He nodded. "Carved it myself. We left part of the stump as a memorial. To remind us how fast things can get out of hand and how important restraint is."

He paused, eyes distant. "I still remember the roar of the chainsaws, the shadows of the choppers. I remember thinking, 'This is what peace through strength looks like."

Lilly swallowed. "Thank you for being there."

Mr. Livsey's eyes glistened. "Thank you for remembering."

Back in the Garage the teens sat in silence, the memory of the meeting still fresh.

Lilly closed her notebook. “Report title: World-War Tree.”

Rose nodded. “Lessons: Sometimes the simplest object like a tree can trigger massive tension.”

Hayden smirked, “And always bring enough troops to cut a tree.”

They exchanged grins as the chronojumper hummed again, ready for the next mission through time.

Frontier Fury

The garage was silent except for the occasional creak of the old house settling and Hayden's restless tapping on the concrete floor.

"So, what's the plan?" Hayden asked, tossing a crumpled-up paper into the trash can.

"We've done nukes, war horses, tree cutting... but I want real battles. Explosions. Strategy. The kind of gangster stuff that makes history actually cool."

Rose adjusted the dials confidently. "Good. Because today, we're meeting the man who rewrote the rules of war before it was even cool Daniel Morgan."

Lilly pulled out her notebook, already scribbling. "A legendary frontiersman, a sharpshooter, and a master tactician. His name is everywhere in the American Revolution."

Rose grinned. "Alright, time to meet history's original gangster general."

Rose picked up the chronojumper, "ALISSA, take us to Winchester, Virginia, on July 15th, 1775."

"Ready for another war." ALISSA responded, "Opening a portal now."

Suddenly, the teens found themselves deep in a dense Virginia forest, early morning mist curling around towering pines and thick brush.

"Whoa," Hayden whispered. "Feels like we're inside a forest... and smells like pine needles."

Lilly nodded. "This is Morgan's world before the Revolution. He wasn't born into fancy uniforms he was a hunter, trapper, and a fighter against Native tribes and British loyalists."

Rose pointed at a rugged, bearded man demonstrating rifle shooting to a small group of settlers.

"That's him, Daniel Morgan. See how he teaches 'aim small, miss small'? He believed one precise shot beats a hail of bullets."

Hayden squinted, watching as Morgan's men moved silently through the underbrush, their rifles ready.

Suddenly, from behind thick bushes, a group of British loyalists appeared.

Morgan raised his hand sharply. The men disappeared into the shadows and trees.

“Hit and run,” Rose whispered. “Morgan’s men weren’t the kind to charge head-on. They struck fast, picked off officers, then disappeared.”

A shower of rifle shots cracked through the quiet. One loyalist dropped.

Hayden grinned, “That’s like modern-day sniper warfare.”

Lilly nodded, “Exactly. Morgan’s frontier experience taught him guerrilla tactics, surprise, stealth, and precise shooting.”

Morgan’s voice rang out, “Stay low, move quietly. The forest is our ally.”

“Transporting you forward to August 6th, 1775, to the Siege of Boston,” ALISSA said as the chronojumper opened a portal.

Rose, Lilly, and Hayden walked through the portal to a rocky ridge overlooking Boston Harbor. British military in bright red coats marched beneath a hazy, smoky sky.

"Welcome to the Siege of Boston," Rose said. "Morgan and his riflemen were part of the Continental Army, ready to give the British hell."

Lilly explained, "Unlike the British, who fought in neat lines, Morgan's men were expert marksmen. They targeted officers, artillery crews, and supply lines."

Gunfire erupted from behind the ridges. The teens ducked instinctively.

"See that?" Rose said, pointing to a British officer clutching his chest and falling.

Hayden said, "Those guys must have hated trying to fight an enemy they couldn't see."

Lilly nodded, "Morgan's men weren't just soldiers; they were hunters. They used trees, rooftops, and rocks to pick off the enemy."

Rose smiled. "The British called them 'the black boys' because of their dark clothing and stealth."

The teens watched as Morgan's sharpshooters fired from cover, spreading chaos among the British ranks.

Hayden muttered, “That’s some next-level guerrilla warfare.”

“Let’s keep moving forward. There’s a lot to see. Transporting you to Saratoga, New York, on August 30th, 1775,” ALISSA said as the chronojumper opened another portal.

Rose, Lilly, and Hayden crossed into the portal to the rolling hills of New York.

“Now, this is where Morgan’s tactics really shine,” Rose said.

Lilly pointed to a battlefield strewn with muskets and smoke. “The Battle of Saratoga, one of the most important turning points in the Revolution.”

Morgan was seen rallying troops, moving from unit to unit, shouting encouragement.

“The British were trying to split the colonies, but Morgan’s riflemen were a thorn in their side,” Rose explained.

Suddenly, Morgan led a daring flanking maneuver, taking the enemy by surprise.

“Here’s the gangster move,” Lilly said. “Morgan used light infantry to hit the British where it hurt, ambushes, sniping, and then falling back.”

Hayden gasped as the battle erupted in full force around them muskets flashing, smoke curling, and soldiers charging.

"Look at how Morgan's men don't just charge, they hit and disappear," Rose said. "That frustrated and confused the British commanders."

Lilly added, "Their patience and precision helped force General Burgoyne to surrender. This victory convinced France to join the war, turning the tide."

"Last stop and also the most dangerous. Transporting you to Cowpens, South Carolina, on January 17th, 1781," ALISSA said as the chronojumper opened another portal.

Rose, Lilly, and Hayden moved cautiously through the portal.

"This was brutal," Rose said. "Morgan was sent south to harass British forces after several Patriot defeats."

The teens saw Morgan training militia, poorly equipped but fiercely determined.

"Militia were tricky," Lilly said. "They often ran at the first sign of trouble. Morgan had to teach them how to hold their ground."

The scene turned tense as British troops approached. Morgan's men prepared an ambush.

"Get ready," Morgan said. "We're going to hit them where it hurts."

The British advanced, but Morgan's riflemen opened fire from behind trees.

Hayden ducked as bullets whizzed past.

Morgan's militia fell back in an organized retreat—just as planned.

Rose explained, "This was all part of Morgan's master plan."

The battlefield cleared, revealing the open fields of Cowpens.

"This was Morgan's biggest moment," Rose said.

Lilly showed her notebook. "He faced a superior British force under Colonel Tarleton."

Morgan laid out his plan: militia in the front, told to fire two shots and then retreat. Veteran riflemen waited behind for the right moment.

Hayden grinned, “Like bait.”

The battle started with smoke and thunder as muskets fired.

The militia fired two shots, then fell back.

The British, eager for victory, charged forward falling right into Morgan’s trap.

Morgan’s veterans and cavalry sprang their ambush.

Bullets tore through the British lines, and cavalry charged from the flanks.

“Cornwallis called Cowpens ‘the perfect battle,’” Lilly said.

The teens watched the British lines collapse under the well-executed trap.

“You survived another war. Taking you home,” ALISSA said as the chronojumper opened a portal home.

Rose, Lilly, and Hayden passed through the portal back to the garage.

Back in the garage, Rose summarized, “Morgan was a rebel who used his knowledge of the land, patience, and smarts to win.”

Lilly added, “He changed warfare, showing how smaller, smarter forces could beat larger armies.”

Hayden laughed, “So yeah, he was the original gangster general.”

Rose smiled. “Exactly.”

“After the war,” Rose said, “Morgan went into politics and helped build the new country.”

Lilly added, “His tactics influenced the U.S. military for generations.”

Hayden grinned, “And his gangster style? Legendary.”

“So,” Rose asked, “what’s the title for this report?”

Hayden said, “Daniel Morgan: The Original Gangster General.”

Lilly laughed. “Perfect.”

Rose nodded, “Let’s hope Mr. Pellicano loves it.”

Hayden raised his hand. “Next stop?”

Rose smirked, “Maybe the Boston Tea Party.”

Hayden asked, “Do they have gangsters there?”

Rose winked. “You might be the only one.”

The chronojumper whirred to life again.

The Last American Uprising

The garage was quiet, the air humming as the chronojumper came to life. Hayden tossed a foam dart into the air and caught it without looking.

"So, what are we looking at this time?" he asked.

Rose tapped the notebook. "Post-World War II America. Small town corruption. And a bunch of veterans who decided they weren't putting up with it."

Lilly smiled. "Welcome to Athens, Tennessee. August 1, 1946."

"Taking you there now," ALISSA said as the chronojumper opened a portal.

Rose, Lilly, and Hayden exchanged a glance before stepping through the portal into the sweltering summer air, standing on a dusty street in front of the McMinn County Courthouse. Banners hung from streetlamps: Election Day.

"This looks normal enough," Hayden said. "People voting, guys in suits shaking hands."

Gunfire cracked in the distance.

"Spoke too soon," Rose muttered.

They ducked behind a parked car as a group of men stormed past, carrying rifles.

Lilly whispered, "Those are veterans. They've just had enough."

Rose explained as they moved through the chaos:

"For years, the local sheriff, Paul Cantrell, and his cronies used voter intimidation, ballot stuffing, and even beatings to stay in power."

"So, like mobsters with badges," Hayden said.

Lilly nodded. “The GIs who came home from WWII saw it for what it was: tyranny. And they’d just fought a war to end that.”

Rose added, “Cantrell was part of a larger political machine known as the Crump organization. It was basically an authoritarian regime at the local level, manipulating elections, misusing funds, and arresting opponents. The veterans believed in the Constitution and didn’t like what was happening.”

Hayden frowned. “Wait, so this was happening after we just fought the Nazis?”

Lilly replied, “Exactly. That’s what made it worse. These men came back expecting freedom and justice. Instead, they found a town ruled by fear.”

The trio slipped into a quiet booth at a corner diner. A group of veterans sat nearby, speaking in hushed tones.

“They’re gonna rig the ballots again,” one vet growled. “They’ve locked up the ballot boxes at the jail. No way they’ll let us win fair.”

“So, what do we do?” another asked.

A tall man with a military haircut stood up. “We do what we were trained to do. We fight.”

Rose leaned to the others. “That’s Bill White. He served in the Pacific. He’s organizing the counterattack.”

Hayden gawked. “He looks like he could take on a tank with a shovel.”

Night fell. The courthouse glowed under streetlights as the corrupt deputies barricaded themselves inside with the ballot boxes.

Shots rang out. The veterans, using M1 Garand rifles, shotguns, and even dynamite, surrounded the building.

“Cover the east windows!” Bill White yelled.

Rose, Lilly, and Hayden ducked near a truck and watched as a group of GIs lobbed a stick of dynamite toward the courthouse door.

Boom!

Smoke and debris filled the air. The door burst open.

“We just want the ballots!” a vet called out.

Deputies fired back.

"They're not giving up easy," Lilly said.

The battle raged for hours. Citizens watched from porches and rooftops, some cheering the veterans on.

Inside, one deputy shouted, "Hold the line! Don't let them take control!"

Another panicked, "We're surrounded! We can't hold this forever!"

More dynamite was thrown. The building shook. Finally, the corrupt deputies surrendered.

Victory!

The veterans stormed inside and retrieved the ballot boxes. They took them to the polling station and began the count publicly and transparently.

"For the first time in years," Rose said, "the people of McMinn County got a real election."

The reform candidates won. The corrupt regime was overthrown without federal help. It was the last time Americans took up arms to fix a domestic election.

Back in the now-liberated diner, the teens listened to the veterans speak.

“The Constitution means nothing if we don’t stand up for it,” one vet said. “We fought for democracy overseas. We weren’t gonna let it die at home.”

Another added, “It wasn’t about violence. It was about principle. We hoped this would never happen again.”

Lilly whispered, “It’s like a warning from history.”

The trio visited the town square the next day. Flags fluttered, people smiled, and a young boy ran past with a newspaper shouting: “GIs Win Back Athens!”

An old veteran leaned on a cane nearby.

“Sir,” Rose asked, “were you part of the siege?”

He nodded slowly. “Yeah. We didn’t want to fight. But we also didn’t want to live under tyrants. We did what we had to.”

Hayden asked, “Was it scary?”

He looked into the distance. “War is always scary. Even at home. But sometimes, if you want freedom, you’ve gotta earn it more than once.”

“Thank you for fighting for our freedom sir” Rose said with gratitude as she and the teen walked away from the vet.

“You just witnessed democracy in action.” ALISSA said as the chronojumper opened a portal home.

Rose, Lilly, and Hayden entered the portal.

Back in the garage, Rose flipped through a history book and added to her notes.

“So, what happened after the smoke cleared?” Hayden asked.

Lilly replied, “The new officials made real reforms, improved law enforcement, opened up public records, and restored voter trust. But the veterans faced backlash from parts of the media and political elites who feared the precedent it set.”

“They were labeled rebels,” Rose added. “Even though they followed the very Constitution they swore to defend.”

The story of the Battle of Athens inspired future generations of veterans and citizens alike to stand up for civil rights. It became a case study in political science and military ethics courses.

“But” Lilly said, “it also became a cautionary tale, a reminder of what can happen when democratic institutions fail and the people are left with no other option.”

Hayden looked serious. “So basically, they became heroes and warnings at the same time.”

Rose nodded. “Exactly. They weren’t trying to start a revolution. They were just trying to end corruption.”

She wrote the final sentence in her report:

"In Athens when the ballot was stolen with bullets. Democracy fired back."

The chronojumper glowed.

Next stop: the Devil Duck, or maybe a duel between senators.

History was full of surprises.

Mallard of Honor

The garage lights flickered as the chronojumper hummed to life.

"Okay," Hayden said, "I'm ready for whatever madness is up next."

Rose smirked. "World War II. Pacific Theater. And yes, there will be a duck."

"You mean like Daffy Duck?" Hayden asked.

Lilly grinned. "More like... a U.S. Marine Corps duck. Codename: Devil Duck."

"That's it, I love history now!" Hayden said, throwing his hands in the air.

Rose grabbed the chronojumper “ALISSA show us the Devil Duck.”

“As you wish.” ALISSA responded, “Opening a portal to Peleliu, Palau Islands, on September 17th, 1944, now.”

Without hesitation, Rose, Lilly, and Hayden plunged into the portal.

The heat was suffocating. Waves crashed against the coral beach, stained by the scars of recent combat. The trio materialized behind a camo net, ducking just as a pair of Marines ran by shouting about ammo.

Then they saw it.

A bright white duck, waddling between crates of grenades and M1 rifles, completely unfazed.

"Is that... it?" Hayden whispered. "That’s Devil Duck?"

"Yup," said Lilly, flipping open her notes. "This little beast arrived on a landing craft during the invasion of Peleliu with the 1st Marine Division. Supposed to be dinner."

"But instead," Rose added, "he became their unofficial mascot."

Devil Duck squawked at a passing corporal, then flapped up onto a sandbag pile like he owned the place.

"He was fearless," said Lilly. "Charged into firefights. Bit military police officers. Attacked anyone who messed with the Marines."

A sudden brawl erupted to their left. Two Marines were shouting at each other over a stolen can of peaches. Devil Duck launched himself off the sandbags and charged in, pecking and flapping until both men backed off.

"He's got more combat missions than half the unit," one Marine muttered, watching the duck strut away.

That night, the teens huddled with the Marines, who were telling stories over tinned beans and warm soda.

"One time," a Private First Class said, "he stole my cigarette right outta my mouth. Just yanked it and waddled off."

"Didn’t like smokers?" Hayden asked.

"Nah, I think he just liked causing chaos."

Another Marine chimed in. "There was that one time during a mortar barrage when he walked across the trench like nothing was happening. Just strutted past us like we were the crazy ones."

Lilly scribbled furiously in her notebook. "They said Devil Duck survived artillery barrages, sniper fire, even a typhoon."

"He followed the Marines from Peleliu to Okinawa," Rose added. "And every time, he came out without a scratch."

"That duck has plot armor," Hayden declared.

Rose, Lilly, and Hayden walked the short distance to Okinawa Beach

As the teens appeared in the middle of an unloading zone, they saw Devil Duck perched triumphantly atop a jeep, wings spread like a general surveying his troops.

"He rode into battle on supply trucks," said Lilly. "And was known to strut around command tents like he owned them."

"At one point, they put a little helmet on him," Rose laughed. "For morale."

Hayden wiped a tear. "I want to be reincarnated as that duck."

Lilly elbowed Hayden in the ribs. “You can’t be reincarnated to the past genius.”

Nearby, a Marine sergeant tried to shoo the duck away from a crate of rations. Devil Duck hissed, pecked the sergeant’s boot, and waddled off in victory.

"Sarge just got owned by a bird," Hayden whispered, eyes wide.

Inside a makeshift bunker one evening, the teens found themselves playing cards with a few off-duty Marines. Devil Duck slept in the corner on a folded American flag.

Suddenly, an alert sounded. Everyone jumped up. The duck awoke, flapping and squawking.

"INCOMING!" someone shouted as a nearby blast shook the ground.

Devil Duck ran straight for the door.

"He’s going out there?" Hayden shouted.

"He always does," a corporal said, grabbing his rifle. "That duck has no fear."

They followed and watched Devil Duck rush out, flapping into the night as tracer rounds lit the sky.

“That’s the end of the Devil Ducks' tour of combat. Time to see what his life was like back home in Camp Pendleton, California. Taking you to October 13th, 1944.” ALISSA said as the chronojumper opened a portal.

Rose, Lilly, and Hayden stepped through the portal.

Back in the States, Devil Duck lived out his days in honor. He had his own fenced yard, a custom water dish, and daily visits from veterans.

"He made it through the war with no official rank," Lilly noted, "but everyone called him Sergeant."

"Because nobody wanted to outrank him," Rose joked.

Local newspapers ran stories. Children visited from the schools. Devil Duck even starred in a few military training films as a morale symbol.

When he passed away, the 1st Marine Division held a memorial service. A bugle played. Veterans saluted. One Marine placed a tiny helmet on his grave.

"He was one of us," a veteran said simply.

ALISSA opened a portal home for Rose, Lilly, and Hayden.

The chrono jumper cooled, gears ticking.

"So, to recap," Hayden said, holding up their report cover, "our sources confirm a duck survived two invasions, assaulted officers, and had a higher kill count than most rookies."

"Report title?" Rose asked.

Lilly grinned. "Operation Devil Duck: One Waddle from Glory."

"Best. Report. Ever," Hayden said.

As the chronojumper began to warm again, Rose glanced at the coordinates. "Next stop, Christmas 1826. Eggnog Riot. Bring a helmet."

"Wait, did you say riot? With eggnog?"

"Yup. And maybe a sword fight."

A Very Rowdy Christmas

“Okay, next stop on our history tour,” Lilly said as she carefully flipped open her notebook and adjusted her glasses with a deliberate seriousness that suggested she was about to unveil something both historical and deeply chaotic. “We’re heading to Christmas Eve, 1826... at West Point.”

Hayden paused mid–candy cane bite, his eyebrows lifting slowly as he processed that combination of words. “Please tell me this involves reindeer, presents, and maybe a snowball fight,” he said cautiously, “and not... war.”

Rose, who was already holding the chronojumper, glanced up with a small grin. “It technically involves eggnog,” she said.

Hayden’s entire posture relaxed as hope returned to his face. “See? That’s festive. That’s wholesome. That’s dairy-based joy.”

Lilly looked up from her notes with a look that suggested otherwise. “Festive, yes,” she replied evenly, “but also criminal, destructive, and completely out of control. It's known as the Eggnog Riot."

Hayden turned slowly. "You cannot riot over eggnog," he said with deep skepticism. "That is physically impossible."

"Oh, they absolutely did," Lilly replied, flipping to a marked page in her notebook. "Cadets at West Point smuggled in whiskey, spiked their holiday eggnog with it, drank far more than anyone with access to military weapons should ever drink, and ended up nearly burning the academy to the ground."

Rose nodded. "We're talking about a military academy full of teenagers," she explained, "where alcohol was completely forbidden and the superintendent was famously strict."

Hayden slowly lowered the candy cane as realization dawned. "So, what you're telling me," he said carefully, "is that this is going to go extremely badly."

"Very," Lilly confirmed. "More than ninety cadets were involved. There were arrests, expulsions, and multiple court-martials."

Hayden gave a small, impressed whistle. "That's... actually kind of impressive."

"ALISSA take us to West Point Academy December 24th, 1826." Rose commanded.

The chronojumper flared to life with a rising hum, light spilling across the garage as a shimmering portal tore open in the air.

The three of them stepped forward and the world snapped into a sharp, biting, icy cold that stole the breath straight from their lungs.

Rose inhaled sharply as frost immediately nipped at her cheeks. “Okay,” she muttered, pulling her jacket tighter around her shoulders, “this is not decorative movie snow. This is real winter.”

Snow crunched loudly beneath their shoes as they appeared on a hill overlooking rows of gray stone buildings arranged with almost unnerving precision.

“West Point Military Academy,” Lilly said quietly, scanning the scene below them. “December 24th, 1826.”

The Hudson River stretched beyond the buildings, dark and smooth like a sheet of black glass reflecting the pale moonlight.

“It looks peaceful,” Hayden admitted, his voice softer now as he watched the stillness below.

Cadets marched across the parade ground in perfect formation, their boots striking the snow in disciplined rhythm. Lanterns glowed warmly inside the barracks windows, casting golden squares of light into the frozen night. Somewhere in the distance, the faint sound of a Christmas hymn drifted through the air.

“This feels completely normal,” Hayden said cautiously.

“It won’t stay that way,” Lilly replied.

Rose nodded thoughtfully. “For context,” she began, “these cadets were basically teenage military college students. Some of them were as young as fourteen years old.”

Hayden turned sharply toward her. “Fourteen?” he repeated. “That’s not a soldier, that’s a child with a musket and pretending to be a soldier.”

"And life here was extremely strict," Lilly added. "Constant drills. Endless inspections. Almost no freedom to do anything without supervision."

"And absolutely no alcohol," Rose said.

"On Christmas?" Hayden asked, stunned.

"Especially on Christmas," Lilly replied. "The superintendent, Captain Ethan Allen Hitchcock, was known for being disciplined to the point of stubborn."

Hayden folded his arms. "So basically, the villain of tonight's holiday episode."

Rose gave a small shrug. "Depends on your point of view," she said. "But tonight, he's about to walk into absolute chaos."

The trio carefully made their way toward the barracks and slipped quietly inside.

The air was immediately warmer, thick with coal smoke and the scent of damp wool uniforms drying near the stove.

But beneath that warmth, there were whispers.

Cadets huddled together near a cast-iron stove, their coats pulled tightly around them, eyes flicking nervously toward the door.

One leaned in dramatically and whispered, "Tonight... we acquire the whiskey."

Hayden's eyes widened with delighted horror. "This is an 1800s holiday heist."

"Eggnog was a traditional Christmas drink," Lilly whispered back. "Milk, eggs, sugar, nutmeg..."

"...and an irresponsible amount of alcohol," Rose finished.

“Dessert soup with life-altering consequences,” Hayden muttered.

They followed from a distance as one cadet slipped into the snowy darkness. Down the road, a wagon waited in the shadows. A barrel was carefully rolled down, coins exchanged quickly.

Hayden stared. “That was literally an 1826 black-market whiskey deal.”

By midnight, the atmosphere inside the barracks had completely transformed.

The stiff, disciplined room from earlier had dissolved into loud laughter and reckless celebration. Cadets crowded around a punch bowl as if it were sacred. Eggs cracked into bowls. Sugar poured in heavy scoops. Whiskey splashed generously and then continued splashing long past too much.

“To the Army!” one cadet shouted, raising his cup high.

Cheers exploded around the room.

“To Christmas!”

More cheers.

“To Hitchcock never finding out!”

Even louder cheers.

Rose winced. “Oh, he is absolutely going to find out.”

One cadet attempted to sit in a chair and missed entirely, collapsing to the floor in a heap.

“How many are drinking?” Hayden asked.

“Dozens,” Lilly replied. “Possibly more.”

“Teenagers plus alcohol plus military weapons,” Rose said under her breath.

Hayden nodded grimly. “Incoming catastrophe.”

A sudden crash echoed from outside the barracks.

Footsteps followed.

Heavy. Deliberate.

Lantern light flickered through the windows.

“That’s Hitchcock,” Lilly whispered.

The door burst open.

Captain Hitchcock stepped inside, and the smell hit him instantly.

His sharp gaze swept the room, taking in the flushed faces, the swaying cadets, the unmistakable evidence.

“Gentlemen...” he said slowly. “Are you drinking?”

Silence felt thick and heavy.

One cadet attempted a salute so aggressive he nearly toppled over. “No, sir!”

Hayden covered his mouth. “That man is both lying and losing the battle with gravity.”

Hitchcock’s expression darkened. “You are all confined to your rooms.”

The tension in the room tightened like a pulled wire.

Someone muttered angrily, “This is tyranny.”

Rose’s eyes widened. “Oh no.”

A bottle suddenly flew across the room and smashed violently against the wall.

For one frozen heartbeat everything stopped.

Then the room erupted into complete chaos.

Cadets surged forward in a wave of drunken rebellion. Furniture overturned. Windows shattered. Shouts filled the air.

“DEFEND THE EGGNOG!” someone screamed.

“They are rioting over dairy products!” Hayden shouted in disbelief.

Chairs flew through the air. A musket fired shooting a bullet into a doorframe, sending wood everywhere.

“This is officially the most ridiculous rebellion in American history!” Lilly yelled as she ducked.

Cadets grabbed swords, muskets, fire pokers, anything they could reach.

“DOWN WITH HITCHCOCK!”

“MORE NOG!”

Rose nearly slipped in a spreading puddle of spilled eggnog. “This is disgusting!”

“WHY IS IT EVERYWHERE?” Hayden yelled.

“Because this is what riots look like!” Lilly shouted back.

Another musket fired.

Rose pulled out the chronojumper. “ALISSA! Open a portal immediately!”

"As you wish," ALISSA responded calmly, as if this were completely routine.

A shimmering doorway appeared at the end of the hallway.

"Run!" Rose shouted.

They sprinted through flying bottles and stumbling cadets, dodging chaos in every direction.

A drunken voice sang loudly off-key, "O Christmas treeeeee..."

"Not the time!" Rose yelled.

They dove through the portal and tumbled back into the warm safety of the garage.

Silence wrapped around them.

Hayden lay flat on the floor, staring at the ceiling. "That," he said slowly, "was the worst Christmas sleepover in recorded human history."

Lilly flipped through her notes. "Over ninety cadets were involved. Many were arrested. Several were expelled. Court-martials followed."

Rose added thoughtfully, "One of those cadets was Jefferson Davis."

Hayden sat upright instantly. "The future President of the Confederacy?"

"Yep," Lilly confirmed. "He didn't get expelled, but he participated."

Hayden stared into the distance. "So, his early career included 'drunken eggnog rebellion.'"

"That... actually makes sense," Rose muttered.

Lilly smiled faintly. "It's a reminder that even future leaders were once reckless teenagers capable of spectacularly bad decisions."

"And that teenagers should absolutely never mix alcohol with weapons," Hayden added firmly.

Rose closed her notebook with a satisfied nod. "Report title: 'The Eggnog Riot: When Christmas at West Point Completely Fell Apart.'"

The chronojumper hummed softly again.

"So," Rose asked, looking at her friends, "where to next?"

Hayden held up his candy cane like a warning. "Somewhere," he said seriously, "with significantly less dairy-based violence."

They all laughed as the portal began to glow once more, ready for whatever chaotic chapter of history awaited them next.

Pirates vs. Presidents

“Okay, next stop on our history report tour,” Lilly said, adjusting her glasses and opening her history textbook. “The Barbary Wars.”

Hayden leaned over her shoulder. “Wait, like, ‘barbecue’?”

Lilly rolled her eyes. “Barbary. As in Barbary Coast, North Africa. Pirates, Hayden. This one’s about pirates.”

“YES,” Hayden pumped a fist. “Finally, some real action. Swords, ships, explosions maybe a monkey?”

“We’re going back to the early 1800s,” Rose said, “America’s dealing with pirate nations. Thomas Jefferson’s the president. The Marine Corps is being established. Does the phrase ‘to the shores of Tripoli’ ring a bell?”

Hayden blinked. "Uh... from the song?"

"Exactly," Lilly said. "We're going to see how the U.S. stopped paying ransom and started wrecking pirate strongholds."

"Three... two... one..." Rose said. The chronojumper opened a portal, and they were gone.

Rose, Lilly, and Hayden exited the portal on May 21st, 1801, on a beach in Tripoli.

The air was dry, the sun blinding. The trio stood on a ridge overlooking the glittering Mediterranean Sea. Below, white-sailed ships floated in a harbor near a city surrounded by high walls: Tripoli.

"This is it," Lilly said. "Tripoli. One of the Barbary States. For decades, they've been seizing ships, taking crews hostage, demanding tribute."

"The Barbary States," Rose explained, "were a group of North African territories Tripoli, Tunis, Algiers, and Morocco. They were part of the Ottoman Empire but acted independently when it came to piracy. Their economies thrived on capturing ships and holding crews for ransom. Most European nations paid tribute to avoid conflict."

"Didn't America just pay them off?" Hayden asked.

"At first," Rose replied. "We were a brand-new country, no navy to speak of. But that changed."

They crept closer to the harbor, staying out of sight. Marines were unloading equipment from ships. Officers shouted orders. One officer stood tall, stern-faced and clearly in command.

"That's William Eaton," Lilly whispered. "He's leading a crazy mission to install a friendlier ruler in Tripoli."

Hayden watched as Eaton and a group of Marines marched into the desert with a diverse group of mercenaries and local fighters.

"Where are they going?"

"To march across 600 miles of desert," Lilly said. "To attack the city of Derna from the land side while the U.S. Navy bombards the coast. It's the first recorded land battle the U.S. fought overseas."

"Wait... they're walking across the desert to fight pirates?" Hayden said. "That's the most American thing I've ever heard."

Rose nodded. "And the pirates had been demanding tribute for years. Jefferson was the first president to say no."

"Not just no," Lilly added. "He also sent the Navy. That was a big deal for a young country barely out of the Revolution."

“Time to get your sea legs.” ALISSA said as the chronojumper opened a portal to the USS Constitution on August 3rd, 1804.

Rose, Lilly, and Hayden jumped though the portal and landed on the deck of the USS Constitution, the legendary American warship.

Cannons roared. Smoke filled the sky. The ship shook beneath their feet.

“This is the bombardment of Tripoli,” Lilly said. “The Navy wasn’t just fighting ships they attacked the harbor itself. They were done playing defense.”

They spotted Stephen Decatur a young naval officer leaping from a rowboat with his men, climbing aboard a burning enemy ship.

“He’s leading a raid to destroy the USS Philadelphia,” Rose explained. “It was captured by pirates. Rather than let them use it, Decatur and his men snuck in and burned it.”

“That’s insane,” Hayden whispered. “They lit their own ship on fire?”

“Better that than let it be used against us,” Lilly said. “It was one of the boldest naval missions ever pulled off. British

Admiral Nelson called it 'the most bold and daring act of the age.'"

Rose grabbed the chronojumper "ALISSA take us to Derna, Libya."

"As you wish," ALISSA responded, opening a portal now.

Rose, Lilly, and Hayden were now outside Derna. Eaton's forces had reached the city.

Gunfire cracked in the distance. Marines advanced through narrow streets. Smoke and dust choked the air.

"This was it," Lilly said. "The Battle of Derna. Eaton, Marines, and mercenaries stormed the city. It shocked everyone."

"They had barely two dozen Marines," Rose said. "But they led a much larger force and captured a fortified city."

The trio ducked behind a stone wall as cannon fire rang out. Marines surged forward with bayonets.

"Did we win?" Hayden asked.

"Oh yeah," Rose said. "Captured the city. Forced the ruler of Tripoli to negotiate. It proved America wouldn't be bullied."

The trio watched as the American flag was raised over a foreign fortress for the first time in history.

“That’s where the line in the song ‘to the shores of Tripoli’ comes from,” Lilly added. “It’s in the Marine Corps Hymn to this day.”

Hayden looked around at the sand, smoke, and sunburned Marines. “You know, I thought this would be about parrots and eyepatches. But this is way cooler.”

“It’s about the U.S. deciding to stand up,” Rose said. “Even when it was risky.”

“And the Barbary States?” Hayden asked.

“They backed off,” Lilly said. “Eventually. There was a second war in 1815, but by then the U.S. had more ships and experience. That time, we really ended it. No more tribute. No more hostages.”

Rose added, “The Second Barbary War was led by Stephen Decatur again. After the War of 1812, the U.S. built a much stronger Navy. Decatur sailed straight to Algiers, captured enemy ships, and forced peace treaties at cannon-point. Algiers, Tunis, and Tripoli all agreed to stop taking hostages. That was the end of the Barbary pirates’ power.”

"They were the first nations we fought after independence," Rose said. "We proved we'd defend our people, no matter how far from home."

"The first Barbary war is over. Are you ready for the second?" ALISSA said as the chronojumper opened a portal to the USS Guerriere off the coast of Gibraltar on June 14th, 1815.

When the teens exited the portal, the salty sea air hit them first as they stood aboard the deck of the powerful American warship. Around them, a fleet of sleek frigates sailed under a clear blue sky, cannons gleaming in the sunlight.

"We're off the coast of Algiers," Lilly whispered. "Stephen Decatur is leading the fleet. After years of paying tribute, America has finally had enough."

Rose added, "The War of 1812 gave the U.S. Navy more experience and ships. Now, they're taking the fight to the pirates. One of the valuable lessons Decatur learned during the War of 1812 was that there is always a way to defeat a larger military."

They watched as Decatur paced the deck, confident and commanding. The ships fired warning shots toward the harbor.

Suddenly, the sound of booming cannons echoed as the fleet opened fire on pirate vessels and fortifications.

Explosions sent water and smoke into the air.

Marines boarded captured enemy ships, seizing weapons and supplies.

"Decatur's mission is to force the Barbary States Algiers, Tunis, and Tripoli to sign treaties ending piracy and hostage-taking," Lilly explained.

Hayden cheered quietly, "Take that, pirates!"

Days later, the teens stood on a shore where diplomats from the U.S. and the Barbary States met.

A large parchment lay on a wooden table, with ink drying on the treaty.

The Barbary leaders, looking wary and defeated, signed the agreement.

Rose read aloud, "They agree to stop demanding tribute and to release all American hostages."

Lilly added, "This treaty officially ended the Barbary pirate threat to the United States."

Hayden grinned. "So, America didn't just defend their boats—they ended piracy in the Mediterranean?"

"Exactly," Rose said. "It was a major step toward the U.S. becoming a respected naval power."

"Congratulations on surviving both Barbary Wars." ALISSA said as the chronojumper opened a portal home.

"It's time to go," Rose said.

Back in Rose's garage, Hayden flopped on the couch.

"New report title: 'America vs. Pirate Nations: Don't Touch Our Boats!"

Rose laughed. "Perfect."

Lilly opened her notes. "Seriously though Decatur, Eaton, Jefferson… this whole episode was the start of America's military power abroad."

"Also," Hayden said, "those Marines were awesome."

Lilly laughed. "This is going to be our best history report yet."

Rose smiled. “Let’s keep exploring.”

Naval Nonsense: The Legend of the Willie D

The chronojumper buzzed and opened a portal with a low mechanical hum. Rose tapped furiously at the keys, navigating historical coordinates and adjusting the era-drift compensation.

“So, what kind of disaster are we walking into this time?” Hayden asked, flopping onto a beanbag and biting into a chicken nugget.

Lilly grinned. “The USS William D. Porter. Or as sailors called it… the Willie D.”

Rose chuckled. “It was a Fletcher-class destroyer in World War II. Its service record? One accident after another. Seriously, it’s like the Navy version of a slapstick comedy.”

“Wait,” Hayden said, perking up. “Is this the ship that almost assassinated the President?”

Rose nodded “It did so much more than just that. It was both the luckiest and unluckiest ship in American history.”

Rose grabbed the chronojumper “ALISSA show us the life of the Willie D.”

“As you wish.” ALISSA responded, “Opening a portal now.”

Rose smiled. “Buckle up we’re hitting the high seas again.”

November 12, 1943 — Departure from Norfolk Naval Yard

They arrived on the deck of a brand-new destroyer as a crisp breeze swept across the water. The hull gleamed in the morning light, marked with the number 579.

Sailors in blue uniforms rushed about, preparing to set sail. Officers barked orders. The harbor buzzed with wartime energy.

“This is it,” Lilly said, grinning. “The USS William D. Porter, setting out for its first big mission.”

From the bridge, a stern-looking man with deep-set eyes and a salt-and-pepper mustache stepped forward.

“Captain Wilfred Walter,” Rose noted. “Experienced, serious, and very proud of his new command. Poor guy didn’t know what was coming.”

Moments later, a thunderous CLANK echoed across the harbor.

A sailor had accidentally dropped the anchor right onto the deck of the USS Clemson docked beside them.

Clemson’s crew erupted into shouting. Sailors from both ships scrambled to check the damage.

“Yup. That’s the first accident,” Lilly said. “They hadn’t even left port.”

Captain Walter’s face tightened. He said nothing, just turned and walked back to the bridge.

The teens shifted forward in time, now watching the Willie D at sea, part of a convoy assigned to escort the USS Iowa, a battleship carrying none other than President Franklin D.

Roosevelt, along with Admiral Ernest King and Secretary of State Cordell Hull.

"High-profile passengers," Rose whispered. "Zero room for mistakes."

"Guess what happens," Lilly added.

Hayden laughed nervously. "Do they run into a whale or something?"

"Worse."

As they watched from the deck, a massive depth charge rolled loose from the Willie D's stern. It hit the water and exploded, sending up a geyser of foam and nearly knocking a sailor off the rail.

Hayden jumped. "DID THEY JUST BOMB THEMSELVES?"

Rose nodded. "They forgot to strap down the depth charges, and one rolled into the water. The Navy took that kind of thing very seriously."

Captain Walter stormed out, barking orders to the crew. His jaw was clenched tight.

"Thankfully nobody was injured and the Willie D was not damaged." Lilly said.

"But." Rose interrupted, "That would not be the only incident on this mission. ALISSA take us to the torpedo incident on November 14, 1943."

"As you wish. Opening portal now."

Th trio walked through the portal onto the deck and stood just behind the gun crews during a "torpedo drill."

Lilly leaned in. "This was a simulated attack. The Willie D was ordered to launch a fake torpedo at the Iowa to practice presidential defense drills."

Below deck, a sailor named Lawton Dawson loaded the torpedo tube.

“What he didn’t realize,” Rose whispered, “was that he had left the primer in, making it a live torpedo.”

Hayden gasped. “That’s like loading a paintball gun with a real bullet!”

Suddenly, there was a WHOOSH!

A white streak flew across the water. The crew froze. One sailor screamed, “We just launched a real torpedo!”

On the Iowa, chaos erupted. The ship zigzagged away at full speed while smoke shells were dropped to obscure visibility.

“No one knew if it was sabotage,” Lilly explained. “Radio silence was enforced because of FDR's presence, so the Willie D had to signal with a lamp.”

Rose winced. “And they accidentally blinked the wrong message first: ‘There is a torpedo moving away from you.’ Not helpful.”

Next, they flashed: ‘We are going in reverse.’ Also, not helpful to the situation.

Finally, Captain Walter decided to break radio silence as he got on the ships radio and yelled “Torpedo in the water!”.

The Iowa radioed back,” Say again.”

Captain Walter got back on the radio “This is the Willie D. There is a torpedo heading straight toward you. Turn now!”

President Rosevelt being the fearless man he was asked his aid to wheel him to the railing of the deck so he could see this torpedo that at the time was screaming toward him.

Thankfully the USS Iowa turned at the last minute and the torpedo exploded harmlessly in the Atlantic.

Not knowing why, the Willie D shot a torpedo at them the Iowa pointed all of its weapons at the ship and ordered it to return to port immediately.

Hayden was pale. "That was almost the worst day in American history."

Back aboard the Willie D, Marines suddenly arrived by boat and climbed aboard with rifles.

"They arrested Captain Walter and his officers," Rose said. "No destroyer captain had ever been arrested in the middle of wartime service before."

"But after an investigation," Lilly added, "it was determined to be an accident, a horrible one, but not sabotage."

Hayden asked, "Did Captain Walter get kicked out?"

Rose shook her head. "He was relieved temporarily but not permanently punished. And the torpedo guy? Dawson?"

Lilly nodded. "He was sentenced to hard labor, but President Roosevelt personally pardoned him."

Hayden blinked. "The guy he almost blew up… pardoned him?"

"Yep," Rose said. "FDR had a good sense of humor and thought it was funny."

The Kamikaze That Missed — June 10, 1945

They shifted forward again. Now the Willie Dee was in the Pacific, near Okinawa.

"It served out the war," Lilly said. "Escort duty, screening carriers. It actually performed well, no major combat losses."

Suddenly, a Japanese kamikaze, badly damaged, spiraled toward the destroyer.

"Brace for impact!" Hayden shouted.

But instead of hitting the ship, the plane crashed just under the waterline, detonating a massive explosion beneath the hull.

The engine room flooded. The boilers failed. The ship began to sink.

“Despite everything,” Rose said, “the crew evacuated with discipline. Not a single man died.”

Hayden was in awe. “So, the ship that bombed itself, dropped an anchor on a neighbor, and almost killed FDR… didn’t lose a man when it finally sank?”

“Exactly,” Lilly said. “Unluckiest ship, luckiest crew.”

“That’s enough ALISSA send us back. I don’t want to catch bad luck.” Rose said while looking at the chronojumper.

“As you wish” ALISSA replied before opening a portal.

Back in the Garage

The chronojumper settled back into place with a soft hiss.

Hayden sat cross-legged on the floor. “I feel bad for Captain Walter.”

“Same,” Rose said. “He was a good officer. Everything that happened was mostly the result of rushed training and just plain bad luck.”

“He tried to turn it around,” Lilly said. “And to his credit, he didn’t let it ruin the crew’s morale. The Willie D became a legend.”

Hayden grabbed the notebook. “New report title: ‘The Destroyer That Couldn’t Catch a Break’.”

Rose smiled. “We’ll make sure people remember Captain Walter and his wild, cursed ship, not just the accidents, but the heart behind them.”

The chronojumper suddenly came back on.

“Where to next?” ALISSA asked.

“How about a hockey game?” Rose replied

The REAL Miracle on Ice

The garage hummed as Rose carefully picked up the chronojumper. Her eyes gleamed with excitement.

“Ready for the fiercest hockey battle of the Cold War?” she asked, a sly grin spreading across her face.

Hayden cracked his knuckles eagerly. “I’m all in, especially if there’s fighting.”

Lilly flipped open her notebook and adjusted her glasses. “This is the 1976 showdown between the National Hockey Leagues Philadelphia Flyers, aka the Broad Street Bullies, and the Soviet Union USSR Red Army team. It wasn’t just a game; it was Cold War politics on ice.”

Rose looked at the chronojumper and said, “ALISSA, take us to the Flyers vs Red army game.”

The teens walked through the portal and found themselves standing just behind the Plexiglas at ice level inside the packed Spectrum Arena.

It was January 11th, 1976, just six months before the American people would be celebrating the countries 200th birthday.

The Flyers skated onto the ice with unmistakable swagger, tough, fearless, and infamous for their brutal physical style.

Dave "The Hammer" Schultz cracked his knuckles, a grin flashing as he eyed the Soviet players across the rink. Bobby Clarke, the gritty and scrappy Flyers captain, barked orders, rallying his teammates. "Protect each other out there, no mercy!"

On the other side, the Soviet Red Army team glided smoothly, a picture of precision and discipline. Valeri Kharlamov, their brilliant forward, surveyed the rink with calm intensity. Defenseman Valeri Vasiliev appeared composed, but the tension was visible.

Lilly whispered, "The Soviets were basically state-trained soldiers on skates, disciplined, precise, with incredible technical skills."

Hayden chuckled, "And the Flyers? Like a pack of street fighters."

The puck dropped with a sharp clang, and the game exploded into a whirlwind of action.

Almost immediately, Schultz charged at Vasiliev. The two collided hard along the boards, and fists flew. Schultz's punches hit like hammers as Vasiliev struggled to shield himself before falling to the ice.

Rose narrated, "Schultz was the Flyers' enforcer. His job was to protect his teammates with intimidation and fists. That first fight set the tone loud and clear."

Lilly added, "The Soviets were used to skill and finesse, but the Flyers played a much more physical, punishing style, something the Soviets weren't ready for."

Bobby Clarke ripped a hard wrist shot from the blue line, catching Soviet goalie Vladislav Tretiak off guard. The puck slammed into the net, and the Flyers took an early lead.

Hayden cheered, "Wow! Clarke's shot was a laser!"

But the Soviets quickly responded. Alexander Yakushev darted between defenders and scored a slick, smooth goal, tying the game.

Lilly noted, "Yakushev was pure skill, fast, elusive, a nightmare to defend."

Tempers began to flare. Clarke and Kharlamov crashed into each other chasing a loose puck. Clarke slammed into Kharlamov with a punishing body check, sending the Soviet star sprawling.

Kharlamov sprang up, face flushed with rage and threw a sharp punch. The two tumbled down in a whirlwind of gloves and fists, trading blows as teammates scrambled to separate them.

Rose said, "Clarke was fearless and relentless, while Kharlamov was graceful on the ice but fiery when provoked."

Schultz kept up his relentless assault, throwing powerful punches and breaking up Soviet plays with sheer force. The Flyers' punishing style rattled the Soviets, who were used to cleaner hockey.

Bill Barber pounced on a rebound and scored, giving the Flyers a 2-1 lead.

Hayden shouted, "Barber's goal was slick! They're mixing skill with brute force perfectly."

Boris Mikhailov, the Soviet captain, tried to inspire his teammates with aggressive plays. He leveled Gary Dornhoefer with a crushing body check, driving him into the boards.

Lilly jotted notes, "Mikhailov was their version of an enforcer, more tactical, but willing to throw down."

After several brutal fights, including Schultz knocking out two Soviet players, tensions exploded. The referees seemed powerless to control the Flyers' violence.

Suddenly, in a stunning moment, the Soviet players skated off the ice mid-game, refusing to continue.

Hayden gasped, “Did they just quit?!”

Lilly explained, “The Soviets protested what they called excessive violence and biased refereeing, and they walked off in protest.”

Rose frowned, “This was more than a game; now it was a Cold War political showdown.”

Back in the locker rooms, the Soviet coaches argued heatedly with officials. Pride, politics, and national honor clashed. The Flyers waited tensely on the ice while the crowd roared.

Finally, after intense diplomatic talks between American and Soviet officials, the Soviets reluctantly agreed to return, but only under watchful eyes.

The Soviet team returned, faces hard and determined.

Kharlamov weaved through defenders to score an electrifying goal, tying the game again.

Then Bobby Clarke answered, crashing to the net and jamming the puck past Tretiak, restoring the Flyers’ lead.

Hayden cheered, “Clarke’s got ice in his veins!”

Near the end, Schultz and Mikhailov faced off in an epic slugfest. Punches flew with wild abandon, helmets and gloves scattered, and both were kicked out, but not before leaving the arena buzzing with raw tension and excitement.

Rose said, “That fight was the climax of a true battle for dominance.”

The game ended 4-3 for the Flyers.

Hayden whooped, “The bullies won!”

Lilly nodded, “It was a victory for grit and guts over precision, but it was also a Cold War message.”

Rose smiled, “With the Soviet Union trying to bully the US in the Cold War the Flyers decided sometimes you have to be the bigger bully.”

With the game over and excitement dying down the chronojumper turned on, “That is all I have from this event.” ALISSA stated before opening a portal back to the garage.

Back in the garage, the teens sat quietly.

Lilly mused, “This game wasn’t just hockey. It was the working-class toughness of America against the state-trained perfection of the USSR.”

Rose added, “Every punch, every fight symbolized decades of political tension.”

Hayden grinned, “The Flyers weren’t just players, they were warriors on ice.”

Rose closed the notebook. “Report title: Broad Street Bullies vs. Red Arm: Cold War Clashes on Ice.”

Lilly smiled. “Mr. Pellicano is going to love this. He mentioned his dad and uncles are a big Flyers fans.”

Hayden stretched. “Next up, the actual Miracle on Ice from 1980?”

Rose laughed. “Maybe next time.”

The 8-Hour Naval War

The chronojumper buzzed with energy as Rose flipped through a history book. "You know what? We are going to go a little off book on this one."

"What do you mean?" Lilly said with a confused look.

"I remember my uncle telling me a story that happened when he was little. It was old enough to be history but not old enough to be in these books" Rose replied.

Hayden jumped in, "You mean in the 1980's? That was a real long time ago."

"Alright," she said, brushing a lock of hair behind her ear. "ALISSA take us to the Persian Gulf on April 17th, 1988."

Hayden perked up. "The '80s? Are we getting big hair and neon jackets?"

"Nope," Lilly said, flipping through her notes with a knowing grin. "We're heading into one of the largest and most decisive naval battles since World War II. Operation Praying Mantis."

Hayden squinted. "Sounds like a kung fu movie."

Rose smirked. "More like a real-world lesson in overwhelming firepower. This is the day that America responds to an Iranian attack by dismantling nearly half of its navy. In only eight hours."

The chronojumper opened a portal and, with a soft hum, they vanished into the chaos of the late Cold War.

Before the guns fired and the missiles launched, there was a lot of it. The teens found themselves momentarily in a secure room inside the Pentagon, the day before Operation Praying Mantis was to happen.

Military officials and White House staff stood around a table crowded with maps of the Persian Gulf. Red pins marked oil platforms and naval bases. Photos from reconnaissance satellites were scattered across the surface.

"The mine that hit the Samuel B. Roberts was Iranian," Navy admiral Anthony A. Less said flatly. "We traced its manufacture and deployment. We can't let this stand."

A civilian advisor adjusted his glasses. "The president wants a proportional response. Nothing that triggers a full war. But it has to hurt."

"We'll hit their oil platforms; they're being used for military surveillance and attacks. Take out their ability to stage these operations."

Another general added, "And if they respond, we target their navy directly. Minimal risk to our people. Maximum impact."

Rose, Lilly, and Hayden watched from the shadows of history.

"They were walking a tightrope," Rose whispered. "Trying to send a message without starting something bigger."

"And planning it down to the last missile," Lilly said.

"Gives me chills," Hayden added. "Like chess. With battleships."

Rose looked at the chronojumper, “ALISSA take us to the main event.”

“Taking you one day into the future.” ALISSA said as a portal opened.

April 18, 1988 – Persian Gulf

The trio reappeared aboard the USS Samuel B. Roberts, where smoke still lingered on the deck from a recent explosion. The heat was stifling, the air was thick with diesel fumes and the sharp bite of burned metal. Sailors moved with urgency, spraying foam and securing bulkheads.

Hayden covered his nose. "What happened here?"

"She struck an Iranian mine three days ago," Rose explained. "It tore a huge hole in her hull. Eight sailors were injured, and it nearly sank the whole ship."

“She?” Hayden asked.

“Many sailors have historically referred to their ships as ‘she’ sometimes affectionately or humorously. Some joked that it’s because ships can be unpredictable.” Rose replied.

Lilly pointed toward the engine room where engineers worked furiously. "The crew kept her afloat by sealing off compartments and fighting fires for hours. They were heroes. But this mine? It was the last straw."

"This is the American response," Rose said. "Operation Praying Mantis. It's happening today."

Suddenly, the deck shook under the roar of jet engines. Above, F-14 Tomcats streaked through the sky, sleek and fast, leaving contrails against the sun.

"Welcome to the war zone," Rose muttered.

The trio shifted to the deck of the USS Wainwright, part of one of three battle groups assigned to strike Iranian targets. Radar screens glowed and sailors barked coordinates.

Rose narrated, "Three separate task groups are moving in simultaneously. First targets: Sassan and Sirri oil platforms."

Through binoculars, they watched Navy SEALs issue warnings through loudspeakers. Workers scrambled to evacuate.

Then came the explosions.

The USS Simpson and USS Bagley opened fire, followed by helicopters launching missiles. Fireballs erupted from the platforms. Smoke coiled into the sky.

"These weren't just oil rigs," Lilly said. "They'd been turned into surveillance and weapons stations. They used them to attack neutral shipping."

"And we warned them first?" Hayden asked.

"Multiple times," Rose confirmed. "They didn't listen."

The structures crumbled into twisted steel.

"That was precision," Hayden said, eyes wide.

Now aboard the USS Simpson, the trio stood near a cluster of sailors staring at radar blips.

"Incoming Iranian Boghammar speedboats," someone shouted.

The teens held onto the rail as the American ships maneuvered, engaging the tiny but dangerous boats. The Boghammars fired machine guns and rockets, but they were no match for coordinated U.S. firepower. Helicopters from the USS Trenton joined in, their door gunners letting loose.

"Small craft down!" someone yelled.

"Multiple kills," another confirmed.

"These boats were attacking merchant ships just days ago," Lilly said. "Now they're part of a shooting gallery."

In the distance, an Iranian frigate, the Sahand, came into view. It moved aggressively toward the U.S. ships.

"Here it comes," Rose whispered.

The Sahand launched surface-to-air missiles at U.S. A-6 Intruder jets. The response was swift and merciless.

The A-6s fired back, dropping laser-guided bombs. The USS Joseph Strauss added a Harpoon missile to the mix.

The Sahand was hit multiple times. Flames burst from her deck. Secondary explosions followed as the ammunition storage ignited.

The frigate leaned to the side. Fire spread across the ship.

Hayden flinched. "That's… brutal."

"It burned for hours," Lilly said. "Eventually sank in shallow water."

"And yet," Rose added, "the Iranians sent another."

The Sabalan, another Iranian frigate, moved in later that day. It fired at a U.S. A-6 patrol.

The Americans answered with a laser-guided bomb that pierced the ship's deck. The explosion didn't sink her, but she lost power and went dead in the water.

"U.S. forces had her dead to rights," Lilly said. "But they didn't finish her off."

"Why not?" Hayden asked.

"Because the message was sent. The U.S. wanted to punish, not provoke full war," Rose replied. "Letting her survive, helpless, was the exclamation point."

By nightfall, the sea was still. Fires smoldered in the distance. The U.S. had destroyed two major oil platforms, sunk or disabled six Iranian vessels, including nearly half their combat-ready navy, and suffered no combat casualties.

The teens stood on the deck of the USS Enterprise, the flagship of the battle group. The horizon glowed orange.

"Operation Praying Mantis was over in just eight hours," Rose said. "But it was one of the most powerful demonstrations of U.S. naval force since WWII."

Lilly added, "It also showed how modern warfare could be swift, calculated, and shocking. Iran backed off immediately."

Hayden looked out at the Gulf. "So... we weren't looking for a war. Just setting a boundary."

"Exactly," Rose said. "And they got the message. ALISSA send us back."

Back in the Present

The chronojumper whirred back to life and dropped the trio into the familiar warmth of Rose's garage.

Hayden collapsed onto a beanbag chair. "That was like watching a video game. Real ships, real missiles, real consequences."

"And a real reminder," Lilly said, "of how fragile peace can be."

Rose scribbled the last notes into the notebook. "Report title: 'Operation Praying Mantis: Eight Hours That Changed Naval Warfare.'"

Hayden raised his hand. "So… next stop, something quieter? Maybe a peaceful protest?"

Rose laughed. "I'm thinking something with flying beavers."

"What!?" Hayden said shocked.

“You’ll see tomorrow. It’s getting late.” Rose replied with a grin.

Hayden and Lilly headed home for the night confused as to what Rose has planned for them the next day.

Operation Beaver Drop

The next day Rose, Hayden, and Lilly met back in Roses' garage still tired from the previous day's adventures.

"After the craziness of yesterday I figured we would start today with a simple trip. No danger, no drama, just data," Rose had said as she picked up the chronojumper. "We need a break from near-death experiences."

Lilly was already packed. Her drawstring backpack was full of essentials: the notebook, a compass, a waterproof pen set, and her well-worn pocket history guide titled *100 Forgotten Events That Shaped America.* She even packed an extra pencil sharpener just in case they got stuck somewhere without electricity. Again.

Hayden was doing jumping jacks in the background.

"I hope there's food in this one," he said between exaggerated hops. "Or horses. Or ninjas. Maybe flying squirrels?"

Rose didn't even look up. "There will be beavers. Just beavers. And parachutes."

Hayden landed and looked confused. "Wait. You said we're dropping beavers?"

Lilly beamed. "Operation Beaver Drop. I remember this! It's the 1948 Idaho relocation program where they literally parachuted live beavers into the wilderness."

Hayden blinked. "Like, they dropped them on purpose?"

"They had to," Rose explained. "The beavers were causing problems in developed areas, and driving them out by truck or horseback was too stressful. The Idaho Fish and Game Department came up with this plan to relocate them to remote areas by air."

“The only thing that I never read was why they had to be dropped out of an airplane. What was so stressful about using a truck or horse?” Lilly questioned.

Rose explained, “Well, it was the middle of the summer and cars didn’t have air conditioning at that time. Also, because of the lack of roads trucks could only get so far before they had to be taken on horseback. The process was very slow and not good for the beavers as they like to stay in water as much as possible to keep cool. Unfortunately, it took a few beavers dying for Fish and Wildlife to find this out.”

Hayden was still scratched his head. "So, you're saying this is gonna be a... beaver drop zone?"

Rose held the chronojumper. "Exactly. We're going to observe it. Quietly. No interference. In and out. ALISSA take us to McCall, Idaho on August 14th, 1948."

“Opening a portal now.” ALISSA responded.

"Best. Day. Ever," Hayden said.

They arrived in a clearing surrounded by tall, wind-whispering pines. The smell of pine needles and damp earth hit them instantly. It was early morning, and the air was cool and still. Birds chirped distantly, and sunlight filtered through the trees like golden confetti.

"Welcome to Idaho," Rose whispered, stepping forward and spinning slowly in a circle. "Summer of 1948."

They crept to the edge of the clearing, crouching behind a fallen log. Below them, men in khaki uniforms were loading large wooden crates onto the back of a rumbling cargo plane. Each crate had stenciled letters:

LIVE BEAVER – HANDLE WITH CARE

"That's Elmo Heter," Lilly whispered, pointing to a man giving orders near the plane. "He's the wildlife officer who designed the whole operation."

Lilly opened her notebook. "He designed special wooden crates that would pop open upon landing so the beavers could escape. And each beaver has its own parachute."

"This is amazing," Hayden said. "Can you imagine being the guy who was like, 'You know what? Let's give that rodent a parachute."

The cargo plane started to roll forward, then lifted off into the clear sky with a low, thunderous rumble.

A few seconds later, the hatch opened.

Out came the first crate.

The parachute deployed with a sharp whoosh, and the crate floated gently downward, spinning slightly as it descended.

"There he goes!" Lilly said. "That's probably Geronimo. He was their main test subject. They dropped him over thirty times before the actual mission."

"A hero among beavers," Hayden whispered reverently.

The crate landed softly in a meadow.

The tension from the parachute's release caused the box to pop open.

Out waddled a round, very calm beaver. He looked around, twitched his nose, and immediately began chewing a stick.

"That little guy just parachuted out of a plane and started his day like it was no big deal," Hayden said. "I want his confidence."

More crates followed. Dozens.

Each one floated down like a pod from a spaceship, and one by one, little beavers emerged from their crates and toddled off into the woods or toward the stream.

The trio watched in awe.

"It's like a National Geographic special falling from the sky," Hayden whispered.

They watched in a stunned silence, filled only by the sound of fluttering parachutes and the distant splash of beavers discovering their new home.

Then something went wrong.

One of the beavers chewed out of the wooden box and was standing on the box as it descended to the ground.

"Oh no," Lilly said. "That one is out of its box!"

"He's just enjoying the view on the way down," Hayden explained.

The jailbreaking beaver then did the unthinkable. About 20 feet off the ground, the beaver jumped.

Before anyone could stop him, Hayden took off running.

"HAYDEN!" Rose hissed. "We can't interfere!"

But he was already halfway down the slope.

The girls groaned and followed.

They reached the crashed crate in moments. Inside, a dazed beaver lay still but breathing.

Hayden was already gently lifting it.

"He's alive," he said. "But he's hurting."

"We have to get him to the stream," Lilly said. "If he stays here, he's vulnerable."

Rose hesitated, then sighed. "Fine. But this never happened."

Using Hayden's windbreaker and some sturdy branches, they created a makeshift sling. Carefully, they carried the stunned beaver through the woods. It was heavier than expected and squirmed just enough to make Rose mutter under her breath the entire way.

They moved slowly, ducking under low-hanging branches and stepping carefully over roots. A squirrel chattered angrily at them as they passed, and Hayden grinned.

"Sorry, buddy. Emergency beaver business."

When they reached the riverbank, the other beavers were already exploring. Some dragging branches, others sliding into the water with plops and splashes. A few had already started constructing what looked like the early stages of a dam.

They laid the injured beaver in the grass.

It sat still for a moment.

Then it twitched.

Then it moved.

With a soft grunt, it dragged itself to the edge of the stream and slipped into the water.

It swam in a slow, determined zigzag.

"He's okay," Lilly whispered, tears in her eyes. "We saved a parachuting beaver."

"I’m basically like my favorite comic book hero, Sparkplug" Hayden said with his hands on his hips doing a superhero pose.

Rose glanced at her chronojumper.

"ALISSA get us out of here before Hayden does anything else." she said. "Get ready."

ALISSA opened a portal and they rushed through.

The last thing they saw was the beaver shaking itself dry beside the stream, then disappearing into the brush.

The garage was quiet again.

The three teens collapsed onto bean bags and blankets.

Hayden sighed dramatically. "I will never complain about hiking in the woods again."

Rose glanced down at her device. "Technically, we violated the non-interference protocol."

"Technically, we changed history. According to my research, that beaver was supposed to die." Lilly said.

"Technically," Hayden added, "I touched history with my bare hands. Fuzzy history."

Rose rolled her eyes," ALISSA how bad did we change history?"

ALISSA responded, "That one beavers survival made no major historical difference, and I wiped all records from the internet of what you did."

"So… I did good then?" Hayden said with a guilty look on his face.

"Not exactly but your heart was in the right place. Thankfully it worked out because of Rose and ALISSA." Lilly replied.

Lilly flipped open the notebook.

She titled the next page: The Skydiving Beavers of 1948.

She smiled. History really was wild.

“Hayden you can’t mess up the next one.” Rose said reading her history book.

“Why is that?” Hayden asked.

“Because,” Rose replied,” We’re going back to war!”

Not Too Old to Fight

"I swear," Hayden groaned, flipping through an already completed coloring book, "if you guys don't hurry up and pick the next destination, I'm drawing a mustache on Abraham Lincoln and calling it art."

Rose smirked, opening her history book. "Then let's ditch Abe and meet some real legends."

On the page, vintage black-and-white photos of weathered American soldiers marching in formation, rifles shouldered and jaws set.

"That," Lilly said, adjusting her glasses, "is the 77th Infantry Division. Average age? Thirty-three when the average age for new recruits was twenty-three. Some had gray hair and arthritis, but they fought harder than anyone."

"Why were they so... old?" Hayden asked.

Rose leaned in. "It started in WWI. The 77th was the first National Army division made entirely of draftees. Mostly New Yorkers, immigrants, construction workers, firefighters, the works. They became the Statue of Liberty Division."

Lilly flipped her notebook open. "They fought in the Argonne Forest in 1918. Brutal trench warfare. Some of those men came back for WWII. When the Army reactivated the 77th in 1942, it brought in older officers and non-commissioned officers. Guys who'd been around. They were an experimental division and the military treated them like it. They trained harder than every other division in the worst conditions."

Hayden raised an eyebrow. "So, they weren't exactly spring chickens, but they knew what they were doing?"

"Exactly," Rose said. "They weren't flashy. They were smart, tough, and mean enough to outlast anything. They even earned the nickname 'The Old Bastards' first by a Marine during the battle of Guam then made official by legendary Marine General Holland 'Howling Mad' Smith."

Haydens face turned pale "This is going to be dangerous isn't it?"

Rose laughed and said, "ALISSA, show us the lives of the 77th Infantry Division during World War II."

"Opening a portal to Louisiana on February, 1st 1943"

The chronojumper dropped them onto a sunbaked training field. Uniforms hung damp on barbed-wire fence posts. Sweat-stained fatigues. A sergeant's voice ripped across the range like thunder.

"You think the Japanese are gonna wait for you to lace your boots, Private?! Move!"

The teens flinched as a squad of older soldiers jogged past. Some had potbellies. One man had a limp. Another sported a handlebar mustache that looked straight out of 1918.

"These guys aren't fresh recruits," Lilly whispered. "They're prior service, older conscripts, reservists."

"Look at him," Rose pointed to a grizzled man balancing a mortar shell like it was a loaf of bread. "That guy's probably fifty. And he could still take down a tree."

"They drilled hard," Lilly said. "Longer marches, heavier packs, night training. The 77th didn't get special treatment. They outperformed younger units."

"They were called up after Pearl Harbor," Rose explained. "A lot of them were fathers, business owners, even WWI vets. And they weren't about to let some kids win the war without them."

A whistle blew. Soldiers hit the dirt. Machine gun fire cracked above the teens' heads. Hayden yelped and dove for cover.

"Live ammo? Seriously?" he shouted.

"That's how they trained," Rose said. "The 77th got ready for jungle warfare by crawling through mud, climbing ropes, and storming mock bunkers. No shortcuts."

One older soldier hauled himself over an obstacle wall and landed hard, coughing but grinning. "Still got it," he muttered.

It was a night drill, mud everywhere, boots sloshing, the distant pop-pop-pop of live rounds echoing through the piney darkness like firecrackers. Fog rolled low along the forest floor. Somewhere in the trees, an officer barked orders.

Two squads of fresh-faced twenty-year-olds, new recruits from a younger division, crept through the underbrush. Camouflage smeared on their faces, adrenaline in their veins, they were ready to "capture" the trench ahead and prove they could keep up with the older units.

Hayden squinted through the dark. "They think they're sneaking up on it."

"Wait for it," Rose said, eyes gleaming.

The lead private lunged over the lip of the trench and froze.

"Uh—"

Suddenly: *SPLOOSH.*

A tripwire snapped, yanking a canvas tarp into the air and dumping a freezing bucket of muddy water directly onto his helmet. He screamed like a banshee. Behind him, another recruit tripped and face-planted in the mud, sending his rifle skittering.

The trench erupted with laughter.

"Surprise!" bellowed a gravelly voice. A row of helmets popped up from behind sandbags, grinning, grizzled, and bone-dry.

The "Old Bastards" had already taken the objective. Hours ago.

One of them, chewing on a cigar stub, waved lazily. "You're late."

Another flicked a flashlight on and off in Morse code: *Nice try, junior.*

"They'd dug in before sundown," Lilly whispered. "Used a lateral entry route through a dry creek bed. Totally silent."

"Then they rigged the place like a haunted house," Rose added. "Cans on strings, pressure-triggered flares, even fake foxholes lined with wet leaves."

A rookie dove for one of those foxholes and instantly regretted it. It was three inches deep and full of brambles. He yelped as thorns tore his sleeves.

"They pulled a reverse retreat, too," Lilly said. "Faked a withdrawal, left footprints in the wrong direction, and circled back behind the tree line."

Hayden watched as one of the old soldiers handed a soaked recruit a towel and a sarcastic pat on the head. "That's just cold," he said.

"Literally," Rose replied.

The drill was called off ten minutes later. The instructors were half-laughing, half-trying-not-to-laugh. The younger squads sulked back to their tents, dripping and humiliated.

The Old Bastards cleaned their gear, told war stories, and didn't break a sweat.

"They won the exercise," Rose said, "by outsmarting and out preparing a bunch of kids who still thought war was about speed and strength."

Hayden shook his head, impressed. "These dudes were *mean.*"

"Meaner than the war they were walking into," Rose agreed. "And smarter than anyone gave them credit for. This was not the end of their training. This was the easy part."

“Easy part? They just had live ammunition flying above their heads! What could get harder than that?” Hayden asked with a confused look.

“You’ll see. ALISSA take us to Camp Hyder Arizona on April 19th, 1943.” Rose answered.

As soon as the teens walked through the portal the Arizona sun beat down like a furnace, turning the ground to cracked clay and the horizon into a wavering blur. Heat shimmered off endless rows of olive-drab tents that flapped in the dry wind. Every breath tasted like dust and sweat.

Rose, Lilly, and Hayden crouched behind a stack of sandbags, watching a line of soldiers march past. Their faces lined and sunburned, their steps steady and sure despite the exhaustion in their eyes.

“Where are we?” Hayden asked while wiping sweat from his face.

“This is Camp Hyder. It’s a pop-up military base in the middle of the Arizona desert about 70 miles northwest of Pheonix.” Lilly answered.

“This is where the 77th really earned their toughness.” Rose replied.

Hayden looked shocked, “They look half dead!”

“They just came back from one of their infamous marches through the desert with barley any water. The ugly truth is not all of them survived the march." Rose said lowering her head in respect.

"They Died?!" Lilly instantly yelled.

Under his breath Hayden said, "I will never complain about having to run the mile at school ever again."

"This training is what really turned the 77th Infantry Division into 'The Old Bastards'." Rose explained. "They even got a service medal for surviving the experience, kind of. The Old Bastards with their dark humor made a medal out of a piece of sandpaper and a broken thermometer. They wore it proudly, but the Department of War never recognized it as an official medal."

Lilly cracked a faint smile. "It's totally something they'd do, though. Laugh in the face of misery. It's kind of their way of saying, 'Yeah, we suffered, but we're still standing.'"

Hayden squinted at the horizon. "So, they survived the desert, made their own medals, and still went to war after that? I'd have just quit right there."

Lilly gave him a look. "You'd quit halfway through the first mile."

He raised his hands in surrender. "Hey, at least I admit it."

Rose grinned, but her eyes were serious. "Those guys didn't have that choice. The desert burned away everything weak in them. What came out of Camp Hyder wasn't just soldiers, it was something tougher. Something the enemy wouldn't be ready for."

Hayden looked at her, half-joking, half-awed. "Remind me never to complain about homework again."

Lilly smirked. "You'll still complain."

He sighed. “Yeah… probably.”

“Enough training.” Rose interrupted, “Lets get to the real action. ALISSA take us to Okinawa May 4th 1945.”

“Right away.” ALISSA said as a portal open into the heart of World War II.

May 1945 – Okinawa, Ishimmi Ridge

The teens reappeared under a bruised sky. The air buzzed with flies and the smell of gunpowder. They crouched beside an infantry company advancing through shattered brush.

"Ishimmi Ridge," Lilly said, her tone carrying a great wonder. "Part of the Shuri Line. The 77th took some of the worst of it."

"Night attack, no lights, no firing until contact," Rose said. "Bayonets only."

They watched the 77th Infantry creep forward, ghosts in the dark. When morning came, they charged up the slope, steel and grit leading the way.

"These old men were relentless," Lilly whispered. "They weren’t supposed to win, but they did."

After fierce hand-to-hand fighting, the Americans secured the ridge. The wounded were dragged back. One older sergeant limped past, blood on his sleeve, face unreadable.

“These guys were so good that Marine Corp General Smith considered them to be honorary Marines, a honor that was unheard of at the time.”

“Let’s meet someone from another unit who made history here,” Rose said.

They materialized near a steep slope, Maeda Escarpment, better known as Hacksaw Ridge. Smoke and gunfire filled the air. A lone medic was dragging a wounded soldier across the jagged ground.

“That’s Desmond Doss,” Lilly whispered. “A Seventh-day Adventist combat medic. He wouldn’t carry a weapon but saved over 70 men in one night.”

Hayden stared. “Wait, the guy with no gun is the one still standing?”

They watched Doss lower soldier after soldier down the ridge with a rope sling, his hands blistered and bloody.

“He kept saying, ‘Lord, help me get one more,’” Lilly added.

“The 77th helped him hold the line the next day,” Rose said. “They called him the bravest man they ever met.”

"They freed civilians, captured caves, and pushed farther than anyone expected," Rose said. "They kept going in Guam, Leyte, and Okinawa."

Hayden blinked. "So age really didn’t slow them down. It just made them harder to kill."

"Exactly," Lilly said. "They had less to prove. More to protect. And they didn’t give up."

The chronojumper buzzed again, and the teens landed behind a broken wall overlooking a network of caves and trenches cut deep into the hillside.

“Third week of June,” Lilly whispered. “The Japanese were running out of supplies. Most were sick, starving, or wounded. Surrender was finally an option.”

“Just not to them,” Rose added grimly.

Below, a translator was waving a white cloth. A captured Japanese officer had just given a message:

"We will surrender to anyone, Marines, medics, Navy. Anyone but the Old Bastards of the 77th."

Hayden squinted. "Why? What did the Old Bastards do?"

"They won," Rose said. "Over and over. No mercy, no hesitation. The stories painted them as monsters in olive drab. Over the course of the war the Old Bastards were responsible for 43,385 confirmed kills but only took 358 prisoners."

"But the Old Bastards weren't stupid," Lilly said. "They'd been around long enough to know fighting wasn't always the best path to victory."

The teens crouched as an older American sergeant with a crooked nose and a thick Bronx accent limped past, chuckling.

"Alright, boys," he said to his squad. "Let's give 'em a show."

The Old Bastards disappeared from the front line on paper. Official reports swapped them with a younger infantry unit. Flags were changed. Patches covered. A truck rolled in with "fresh-faced replacements" to "negotiate surrender terms."

But the truck bed was filled with mud-covered, grizzled veterans in new uniforms.

One of them, clearly in his fifties, patted a fake Private First Class name tag sewn onto his chest and smirked. "Look at me. I'm green as grass."

"They posed as another unit?" Hayden asked, wide-eyed.

"Yep," Rose said. "It was part theater, part strategy."

A Japanese officer emerged slowly from the caves, his hands up, scanning the Americans nervously.

"These men," he said, "they are not the 77th?"

"No, sir," said the Bronx sergeant in his best southern accent. "Just farm boys from Iowa. We wouldn't know a Bastard if he bit us."

The Japanese hesitated, then dropped his sword. Dozens followed.

Once the prisoners were disarmed and processed, one Japanese soldier caught a closer look at one of the Americans, his missing finger, his sun-creased face, the unmistakable 77th tattoo just under a rolled sleeve.

His eyes widened in shock. “You… you are the Old Bastards…”

The sergeant laughed. “Guess you boys surrendered to the Old Bastards after all.”

“I think we’ve gotten enough here let’s go. ALISSA take us back.” Rose said looking exhausted from the adventure.

“As you wish.” ALISSA replied.

The teens walked through the portal back to the garage.

"Okay," Hayden said, flopping onto a beanbag, "Lincoln’s mustache can wait. That was epic. Those were the coolest old guys ever. Sucks they weren’t able to officially have the Camp Hyder Medal."

“It’s okay” Rose replied, “Over the course of the war the Old Bastards received a total of 4,846 official medals. Six of the men earned the Congressional Medal of Honor, the highest medal you can earn.”

“I guess that makes up for it but that Camp Hyder metal is cool or hot I guess.” Hayden remarked.

Rose smiled. "Report title: Old Age and Treachery – How the 77th Beat the Odds."

Lilly was already writing. "We should call it The Ghost Division. Because they weren’t loud. Just unstoppable."

Hayden stretched. "Next stop? Hopefully, one without bayonets. Or bugs."

Rose looked at the chronojumper. "We’ll see."

Rampage on Main Street: The Killdozer

The chronojumper flickered with a low hum as Rose looked over a piece of paper "Small town, Colorado. Early 2000s. And we're not going to a battlefield this time."

Hayden tilted his head, curious. "Then what are we doing? This isn't a war story, right?"

Lilly pulled up a grainy image on her tablet: a massive bulldozer, completely covered in metal plating, like a tank. "We're going to meet Marvin Heemeyer."

Rose's face grew serious. "This isn't just about machines or destruction. It's about a man who felt unheard and how far someone can go when they think the system has failed them."

Haydens voice turned somber, "I know that feeling sometimes."

Lilly hugged Hayden, "We all do but this is the story of how not to handle the hard times that come with life."

"This is getting depressing." Rose said while trying to hide her emotions, "Let's just go. ALISSA take us to Granby, Colorado on June 4th, 2004."

"Opening a portal now" ALISSA replied.

The teens visited Marvin's muffler shop, a small, cluttered building with old tools and a dusty workbench.

They watched from a distance as an older man with gray hair and overalls paced nervously in the back room.

"He was a talented welder," Lilly said, eyes wide with respect. "But he felt pushed out by the town council. Zoning laws changed, his land was blocked from expansion, and he kept losing court battles."

Rose added, "He believed the system was rigged against him, like no one cared about his side. So he built the killdozer as a last stand."

Hayden frowned. "So, he just... built a tank and went on a rampage?"

"Yeah," Lilly said softly. "But it wasn't a mindless attack. He planned every detail."

"Now to see what he did with the killdozer. ALISSA open a portal for later in the day."

"Right away Rose. Opening now."

The teens stepped out of the portal and onto a quiet Main Street nestled between rugged mountain peaks. Birds chirped, a soft breeze stirred dust along the pavement, and for a moment, it seemed peaceful.

Then came the rumble.

They turned sharply and saw it: a Komatsu D355A bulldozer, wrapped in thick gray steel plates, moving slowly but unstoppable, like a mechanical beast. The sun glinted off the improvised armor.

"That's the killdozer," Lilly whispered, her voice barely audible.

Hayden blinked, incredulous. "That's a real thing? Like, someone actually built that?"

Rose nodded. "Marvin Heemeyer spent over a year secretly turning this bulldozer into an armored tank. Steel plates sandwiching concrete, bulletproof glass, cameras, air tanks... He was ready for a war of his own."

They ducked behind a parked truck just as the killdozer smashed through the side of a hardware store. The bricks crumbled, and dust erupted into the air.

Earlier that day,

The rumble grew louder as the killdozer approached the town center. The massive machine looked like a beast armored for war, its gray steel plates reflecting the harsh Colorado sun. Dust swirled in its wake.

From a nearby rooftop, Rose, Lilly, and Hayden watched with a mix of awe and dread.

"There it is," Lilly whispered, pointing. "The killdozer is heading straight for the town hall."

Hayden's eyes widened. "Isn't that where the mayor works? What if he's inside?"

Rose shook her head firmly. "Marvin made sure no one was inside. He didn't want anyone hurt. Just to make a point."

The bulldozer's blade smashed through the brick wall of the town hall with a terrifying crunch. Clouds of brick dust exploded outward, coating the street and the teens in gritty gray powder.

Lilly grimaced, coughing. "The sound alone... It's like a freight train wrecking a building."

Sirens blared in the distance as police cars screeched to a halt, officers rushing to intercept.

ping, ping, ping, ping

Bullets rattled against the steel armor of the killdozer, harmlessly bouncing off. One officer fired a flashbang grenade, tossing it into the machine's cooling vent, hoping to disable the operator.

Hayden covered his ears. "Did that work?"

"Nope," Rose said. "The armor was too thick. Marvin had planned for everything."

The machine lurched forward, crushing a parked car beneath its tracks. The metal frame groaned as the car's roof collapsed like a house of cards.

"Look at that," Lilly said, voice tight. "Marvin's destroying symbols of authority: the town hall, the newspaper office, the concrete plant."

Rose's eyes narrowed. "Each one owned or controlled by someone he blamed for ruining his business."

Suddenly, the killdozer smashed into the office of the local newspaper. The windows shattered, sending glass raining down onto the street below.

Hayden gasped. "The paper! Wasn't that the place that reported against him?"

Lilly nodded. "Yeah, they ran stories about his zoning fights. Marvin wanted to silence those voices."

The roar of the engine filled the air, mixed with the cracking sounds of splintering wood and crumbling stones. Dust coated the town like a gray blanket.

From their vantage point, the teens could see police officers taking cover behind vehicles, exchanging tense glances.

"Do they have any plan?" Hayden asked, worry creeping into his voice.

Rose frowned. "It's hard to stop a tank when bullets don't work. They're trying to disable it, but they're almost helpless."

Suddenly, the killdozer turned toward a concrete plant — the place Marvin claimed caused him harm by blocking access to his property.

The massive machine barreled through a wall of concrete blocks. Dust exploded again, blinding anyone too close.

Hayden swallowed hard. "How long can this go on?"

"Not forever," Rose replied. "The machine weighs over 100 tons. It's slow, but unstoppable."

The killdozer crushed more cars, flattened fences, and tore through the streets, carving a trail of destruction.

Lilly's eyes started tearing up. "Millions of dollars in damage… but still, no one hurt."

"That's the weird part," Hayden said, voice trembling. "It's like he wanted to punish, but not kill."

Rose nodded slowly. "A strange kind of justice, raw, painful, and impossible to ignore."

The police tried everything, spike strips, flashbangs, even aiming at the tires, but the machine kept moving.

Finally, after hours of destruction, the killdozer reached the hardware store.

With a terrible grinding noise, the machine's blade broke through the front wall, but suddenly, the ground beneath it gave way.

The killdozer began to sink into the store's garage, smoke rising from the engine.

Hayden whispered, "Is that it? Is it stuck?"

Rose nodded, eyes locked on the scene. "Yes. Marvin's killdozer had finally met its match."

The teens exchanged heavy looks, the silence between them filled with a mix of relief and sorrow.

Later, the teens slipped inside the muffler shop where Marvin's plans and journals were scattered across a desk.

Lilly picked up an old tape recorder and pressed play.

A gruff, calm voice filled the room. "I was always willing to be reasonable, until I had to be unreasonable. This is not vengeance. This is a last resort."

Hayden's eyes flickered with sympathy. "He really believed he had no other choice."

Rose nodded. "That's the tragedy. He felt trapped, unheard, invisible to the people supposed to protect his rights."

A grinding noise echoed in the distance. Smoke rose near the hardware store.

"That's it," Rose said quietly. "The killdozer got stuck. Marvin couldn't get out."

Hayden's voice dropped. "He took his own life inside."

The police spent hours cutting through the armor to reach him, using blowtorches and heavy tools.

"We've seen enough. Let's go." Rose said with a heavy heart, "ALISSA take us home."

"Right away" ALISSA replied.

The garage felt heavy as the chronojumper powered down.

Lilly exhaled slowly. "This wasn't just about a machine or destruction. It was a man's desperate cry for justice."

Hayden shook his head. "But was it justice? Or just chaos?"

Lilly tapped her pencil against her notebook. "It raises big questions: When does protest cross the line? When does the system fail so badly that people feel pushed to extremes?"

Rose added thoughtfully, "And what could have been done differently to hear him before it got this far?"

Hayden whispered, "At what point does the world finally listen?"

Rose flipped her notebook open, jotting down thoughts.

"Marvin Heemeyer's story is a chilling example of what can happen when people feel helpless when laws that were meant to protect us actually hurt us instead."

Lilly leaned in. "It's a modern-day David versus Goliath story except David built a tank instead of picking up stones."

Hayden smirked, "Yeah, except David didn't smash a whole town."

Rose sighed. "It wasn't heroic. It was tragic. But it also forces us to look at how systems can fail people, and how desperation can turn into destruction."

Lilly added, "In the aftermath, towns like Granby tightened zoning laws, increased community engagement, and looked for ways to prevent this kind of alienation."

Hayden nodded. "Justice isn't just about laws, it's about listening and fairness."

The teens sat quietly, the image of the steel-encased bulldozer lingering in their minds.

Rose finally smiled, breaking the silence. "Report title: Justice in Steel: The Story of Marvin Heemeyer and the Killdozer."

Hayden laughed. "I'll never look at a bulldozer the same way again."

Lilly grinned. “History is full of unexpected stories sometimes, the machine tells the story of the man.”

The chronojumper pulsed again, humming with possibility.

“Ready for the next adventure?” Rose asked.

Hayden threw a thumb over his shoulder. “Wherever. Just no more killdozers, please.”

The Most Polite Invasion in History

Rose tapped rapidly on the chronojumper's shimmering control pad.

"Alright, today's stop: Guam. Year 1898. Middle of the Spanish-American War."

"Sweet," Hayden said. "Cannons, sabers, epic battles, here we come!"

Rose raised an eyebrow. "Don't get your hopes up. This is actually one of the most... peaceful invasions in American history."

"Peaceful?" Hayden frowned. "Then why are we going?"

Lilly smiled, flipping through her notebook. "Because it's hilarious. Imagine invading a whole island and the other side doesn't even know there's a war going on."

Hayden blinked. "Wait... what?"

"You'll see," Rose said. "ALISSA open a portal for the USS Charlston on June 21st, 1898."

“As you wish.” ALISSA responded.

With a whoosh, ALISSA opened a portal, and the trio vanished into the past.

The teens materialized aboard the USS Charleston, its massive guns lined up like metal dragons. Sailors bustled across the deck, preparing for what they assumed would be a hostile takeover.

Rose pointed to the approaching green blur on the horizon. “That’s Guam. Spanish territory since the 1600s. But communications are down. The governor there doesn’t even know Spain and the U.S. are at war.”

“That’s... kind of a big thing to miss,” Hayden said.

“Yup,” Lilly added. “Their telegraph cable had snapped weeks ago. No news. No updates. No clue.”

The crew of the Charleston had just arrived from Hawaii, escorting three transports loaded with supplies and U.S. troops. Their orders had been sealed and dramatic: capture Guam on your way to the Philippines. Nobody expected it to be easy.

As the Charleston pulled into Apra Harbor, the ship’s guns fired three booming warning shots toward the island’s main fort.

“Boom!” Hayden yelled, pumping his fist. “Now we’re talking!”

But… nothing happened.

No return fire. No alarms. No scrambling soldiers.

“Did they just... ignore that?” he asked.

“They thought it was a salute,” Rose said, stifling a laugh. “They believed the Americans were honoring them with a naval greeting.”

“I... I can’t,” Hayden said. “This is already the dumbest war ever.”

Back on the dock, the teens spotted a loud man in suspenders and a sun-faded hat shouting over a folding table full of random junk.

"Frank the Merchant," Lilly whispered. "An actual historical figure. Real name is lost to time, but he lived here, sold everything, and knew everyone."

"I got coconuts, I got rum, I got a monkey named Enrique, he juggles!" Frank bellowed to a crowd of sailors.

A wide-eyed soldier handed over two silver dollars. Frank grinned, shoved a tiny cap on the monkey's head, and tossed Enrique into the man's arms.

Hayden doubled over. "That monkey just got drafted."

"He'll probably outrank Hayden by lunch," Rose muttered.

"Frank also tried selling the Americans maps of the island," Lilly added. "Hand-drawn. Some were accurate. Some were… creative."

Rose grinned. "He even offered to translate the surrender for them."

The soldiers went back to the boat while Frank went off to get the Spanish.

A few hours later, a tiny wooden rowboat drifted out from the shore. Inside were Spanish officers in full dress uniform, smiling, waving, and holding wine, cigars, and fruit.

"They brought us snacks," Hayden whispered. "After we shot at them."

One of the officers stood and bowed politely. "On behalf of the governor of Guam, we welcome you to our peaceful island!"

Captain Henry Glass blinked. "Gentlemen... we're at war."

The officers froze. "What?"

"Yes. Spain and the United States are currently engaged in hostilities. Guam is now under U.S. control."

The officers stared in stunned silence. One of them nearly dropped the wine bottle.

"...May we have until tomorrow to pack?" one asked sheepishly.

The next morning, the Spanish garrison assembled, marching slowly, solemnly, but without resistance. There were no shots fired, no raised voices, no arguments.

The governor, too ill to come himself, sent his regards from his bed. "I apologize for being unaware of the conflict," his note read.

The Americans raised the U.S. flag over the island as the Spanish troops quietly boarded a ship bound for the Philippines.

"That's it?" Hayden asked. "We just showed up, fired a few warning shots, and they thanked us?"

"Pretty much," Rose said. "This is what happens when your telegram cable breaks."

"They were so polite," Lilly added. "Even in surrender, they were apologizing."

The Spanish troops had only about 54 men stationed there. Most of their rifles were outdated or unusable. Their coastal fort's cannons had been rusting under the tropical sun for decades. Guam, it turned out, was completely unprepared for any sort of defense.

Interestingly, once the Americans officially took control, they offered to transport the Spanish garrison to the Philippines as prisoners of war. The Spanish accepted with gratitude. The U.S. even let the governor keep his sword, an old-world gesture of honor. Some Spanish officers were allowed to keep their personal effects, and many of them expressed surprise and even relief that things had ended without any bloodshed. They had feared something much worse.

Letters were written, gifts were exchanged, and the entire event resembled a strange kind of diplomatic party more than a military occupation.

As the teens walked through the small village near the harbor, they saw life going on as usual. Islanders traded fruit, fanned themselves under palm trees, and chatted in Spanish.

Rose pointed toward the fort. "They didn't even have working cannons. The defenses were symbolic at best."

"Symbolic?" Hayden asked.

"More like decorative," Lilly replied. "Their powder was probably wet. Even if they'd known about the war, they couldn't have done anything."

The streets were peaceful, filled with the smells of roasted breadfruit and salt air. Children played with palm-frond toys while their parents gathered at market stalls. It didn't feel like an invasion. It felt like a Sunday.

Hayden tilted his head. "So, we're the invaders… and we're the only ones surprised it worked?"

Rose nodded. "Pretty much. Captain Glass followed the protocol, but even he probably couldn't believe how smoothly it went."

With the Spanish officers arrested and shipped off to the Philippines, the Americans turned to the only local who spoke English and wasn't terrified of paperwork.

Frank.

"He knew everyone," Rose explained. "Had maps, spoke three languages, and owned half the supply chain."

"They asked him to help coordinate the transition," Lilly said. "Frank said sure, and by the time anyone noticed, he was calling town meetings, assigning jobs, and printing IOUs with his own face on them."

Hayden nearly fell over. "He made himself king?!"

"Governor," Rose corrected. "Temporarily. But yeah, the people liked him. He lowered rum prices, outlawed siesta taxes, and let Enrique raise the flag."

Cue Enrique, the monkey, clinging to the pole as a tiny American flag flapped behind him.

Lilly added, "It's also important to remember the native Chamorro people had no say in any of this. They were just passed from one empire to another."

"They've seen Spanish flags, now American ones," Rose said. "And in the future, Japanese. Then back to America. The people of Guam have had a rough ride."

The kids stood silently for a moment, the weight of history pressing down on them.

"On that somber note, ALISSA open a portal back to the present." Rose said trying to act sarcastic.

Back in the garage, the chronojumper powered down with a soft hum.

Hayden collapsed into the beanbag chair. "Alright. I've seen shootouts, sea battles, and revolutionaries. But that... that was the most absurd war story yet."

"Report title?" Rose asked.

Hayden grinned. "The Mango War: How America Won an Island with Wine and Manners."

Lilly added, "It shows how war isn't always blood and chaos. Sometimes, it's just bad communication and great timing."

Rose tapped the chronojumper's side. "So... ready for one more naval adventure?"

"Please," Hayden said. "As long as there are engines on the boats."

Grand Theft U-boat

“I’m telling you, we should do aliens in Roswell,” Hayden said. “That’s history and conspiracy.”

“Or we could do something real,” Lilly countered.

Rose looked up from her device. “Real and unbelievable.”

She opened her history book to show an image of a submarine.

Hayden squinted. “That better not be a boat sinking like the Titanic.”

Rose grinned. “Nope. This one’s about the time we robbed the Nazis.”

She turned the page to show a grainy black-and-white image of a German submarine. A swastika flag flew from its tower.

"That's a Nazi U-boat," Lilly said, leaning in. "Captured by the U.S. Navy during World War II."

"Okay… cool," Hayden said slowly. "But how does that beat 'Roswell aliens'?"

Rose grinned. "Two reasons. First, because it’s a REAL story. Second, because we didn't just capture it. We towed it up the Mississippi River and stuck it in Chicago."

Hayden blinked. "We put a Nazi submarine in a landlocked city?"

Lilly grabbed the notebook. "You better believe it."

"Buckle up," she said. "We're going to see how U-505 went from the middle of the Atlantic to the middle of Illinois."

Rose picked up the chronojumper, "ALISSA take us to see the time the US Navy stole a German U-boat."

"Taking you to the USS Guadalcanal in the Atlantic Ocean off the coast of Africa on June 4th 1944"

The teens appeared on the deck of the USS Guadalcanal, an escort carrier slicing through rough waves. Alarm bells rang below deck. Sailors sprinted toward anti-submarine positions.

"That's Captain Daniel V. Gallery," Lilly whispered, pointing to a man shouting orders. "He led the task force that captured the U-505, the only enemy ship the U.S. has captured at sea since the War of 1812."

"They captured it before D-Day," Rose added. "The Navy kept it a secret so the Germans wouldn't realize we stole their codebooks and encryption devices."

"We have it on radar!" a sailor shouted, "Deploy the hedgehog!"

A small rectangle box opened on the deck and launched about a dozen bottle shaped bombs into the air before they dove into the water.

"Radar shows we missed but we definitely rattled her!" the sailor continued, "Drop the depth charges to finish her!"

Suddenly, there was a loud BOOM.

An explosion rocked the starboard side. A black shape broke the surface, the U-505, damaged, leaking, and surrendering.

"She's surfacing!" Rose yelled over the wind.

"And flooding," Lilly added grimly. "The Germans set her to sink the second they abandoned ship."

U.S. destroyer circled. The order came through: "BOARD HER."

“They are going to go inside a sinking submarine?!” Hayden said, shocked by what he was seeing.

“Yup,” Rose said with a grin.

A small boat raced through the water. A group of Navy sailors jumped aboard it, most of them volunteers. At the front stood a thin officer with intense eyes: Lieutenant Albert David.

"That's him," Lilly whispered. "He's about to lead one of the gutsiest operations in naval history."

The motorboat slammed against the sub's hull. Waves crashed. With no time to lose, Lt. David and his men climbed the conning tower and dropped down into a sinking enemy vessel.

“The Nazis are just going to watch them?” Hayden asked watching the Nazis sit in their life rafts.

Rose replied, “They didn’t have a choice. As soon as they surfaced, they surrendered and they didn’t think anyone could steal their sub after what they just did to it.”

Hayden started to look worried, “Oh no what did they do?”

“You’ll see” Rose said with a grin.

The teens followed using the chronojumper and reappeared inside the sub. It was dimly lit, making creaking noises, and flooding fast.

Rose covered her nose. "Oil. Saltwater. And something burning."

Hayden's eyes went wide. "This place is like a horror movie."

Steam hissed from ruptured pipes. Wires sparked. Water poured in from scuttling valves.

"They didn't just open valves," Lilly said. "They also rigged explosives, smashed gauges, and left everything set to 'chaos.'"

"They didn't know the layout," Rose added. "They were guessing, prying open panels, flipping switches, slamming watertight doors."

One sailor jammed a pipe wrench into a valve and forced it shut. Another stuffed a jacket into a gushing pipe.

"The engine was still running," Lilly said. "The sub was literally spinning in circles, half-submerged."

A sailor climbed the tower and sliced the fuel line, choking the engine into silence.

"They worked in freezing water, total darkness, no German translators," Rose said. "Just guts and guesswork."

Lt. David and his crew spent nearly an hour fighting to stop the sub from sinking. They threw out explosive charges meant to sink the sub, sealed compartments, and finally stabilized the sub.

"Lieutenant David got the Medal of Honor," Lilly said. "The only one awarded in the Atlantic during the war."

Hayden whistled. "So we stole a Nazi sub… while it was trying to sink itself… and somehow didn't die."

"Yup," said Rose. "And then it got even weirder. ALISSA take us to the Bermuda Triangle on June 10th, 1944."

“The Bermuda Triangle!?” Hayden gasped.

Lilly put her hand on Haydens shoulder, “Don’t worry. The Bermuda Triangles not real. I don’t think.”

The teens exited a portal to a quiet Royal Navy base in Bermuda. The U-505 floated under tarps. Guards patrolled the perimeter.

"No press. No photos," Rose said. "They didn't want the Germans to know we had it."

"They hid the crew, too," Lilly added. "Kept them isolated so their families couldn't report them as alive."

Hayden blinked. "So, Berlin thought they were all dead?"

"Exactly," said Lilly. “They didn’t even call it a U-Boat or U-505. They referred to it as the SS Nemo which is Latin for ‘nobody’. Kind of an inside joke for the people that knew what was under the tarp.”

“Inside the U-505 is where it gets real interesting” Rose added “While searching the captains office the sailors found a bunch of secret information about the Nazis on paper that dissolves when it gets wet and an Enigma machine.”

Hayden looked puzzled, “Enigma machine?”

Lilly explained, “It was a code-based machine used by the Nazis to communicate where they could change the code whenever they thought the codes were broken. The Germans think U-505 is in the bottom of the Atlantic which meant they didn't change the Enigma codes. And the Allies used the captured data to crack German naval messages for months."

“Okay, so we got the Sub and took it back to the US. Was that the end of it?” Hayden asked.

“Not quite.” Rose said with a chuckle, “ALLISA take us to May 7th, 1945.”

They were in the same place, but now reporters swarmed the shipyard. U.S. sailors posed next to the weathered sub. The secret was finally out.

“What happened?” Hayden asked.

“After Germany surrendered and ended the war in Europe, the U.S. was finally able to tell the secret they had been keeping for almost a year,” Rose replied.

“Why even tell anyone?” Hayden asked.

“They used the press to get support for the war against Japan,” Lilly said. “We took U-505 to all the major ports on the East Coast and charged people to tour it. It was a great way to raise money for the war.”

“They had to raise money for the war,” Hayden said, shocked at the idea the military would be asking for money.

“It was a different time,” Rose added. “The military didn’t have the money it does now.”

“After Japan surrendered, the government didn’t know what to do with it. They even thought about dropping nuclear bombs on it for science — until Admiral Gallery put a stop to that plan,” Lilly continued.

“Finally, they offered the sub to museums,” Rose said. “And Chicago said yes.”

“Why Chicago?” Hayden asked.

“Because they had the space,” Rose answered, “Lets watch them move it to the most landlocked major city in America. ALISSA take us to St. Louis, Missouri on July 4th, 1954.’

“As you wish Rose.”

They emerged from the portal on the banks of the Mississippi River. In front of them, the U-505 was strapped to a floating drydock, tugboats guiding it upstream.

"2,500 miles," Rose said. "From the Gulf to Lake Michigan. Through locks, canals, and cheering towns."

"They still had the swastika on it," Lilly said. "Kids threw rocks. Crowds cheered. It was like a victory parade."

“This is the best way to celebrate Independence Day.” Hayden said before joining the other kids in throwing rocks at the swastika.

A sailor told a local reporter, "We figured if we got it this far, might as well drag it through Missouri."

Hayden laughed. "This is the stupidest genius thing I've ever seen."

“Have you had your fun? It’s time to go back.” Rose said to Hayden, “ALISSA take us home.”

A portal opened and the teens walked through to the garage. The chronojumper powered down. River mud and machine oil still clung to the air.

"This is the only German U-boat ever captured by Americans," Lilly said.

"And the only one turned into a school field trip," Hayden added.

Rose nodded. "It's a trophy, a warning, and a history lesson all in one."

Rose snapped her pencil. "Report title: The Great Submarine Heist of 1944."

"Or," Hayden said, "Grand theft U-Boat."

Lilly laughed. "I think Mr. Pellicano would like that one better."

Rose put down the chronojumper, "Next stop?"

Hayden raised his hand. "Someplace with less water. I’m starting to get seasick."

Rose grinned, “I got just the place.”

Atomic Blasts & A Manhole Missile

Rose stood holding the chronojumper in her hand, "No more seasickness Hayden. We're going to see nuclear bombs explode."

Hayden, peeling open a bag of chips, glanced nervously. "Nuclear bombs!? Like, actual explosions? Are we sure about this?"

Rose, already typing coordinates, smiled confidently. "It's history, Hayden. The truth about America's wildest nuclear tests. Operation Plumbob, 1957."

Lilly adjusted her glasses, flipping open her notebook. "One of the biggest series of tests ever. And some of the craziest."

"Oh great. These nukes are actually exploding." Hayden said, tossing a chip in his mouth, "Lead the way, fearless leader."

"ALISSA take us to the Nevada desert outside of Las Vegas on May 22nd, 1957." Rose said confidently.

The teens walked through the portal to find themselves in May of 1957, standing on dusty desert soil beneath a vast blue sky. In the distance, flat-topped mesas framed the horizon.

“That’s the Nevada Test Site,” Rose explained. “Where Operation Plumbob took place. Over 20 nuclear detonations in five months.”

A low rumble echoed. Suddenly, a gigantic mushroom cloud blossomed on the horizon, towering and glowing.

Lilly pointed to a cluster of scientists behind a protective fence, scribbling notes and snapping photos. “They monitored everything: blast power, radiation, fallout.”

Hayden rubbed his neck. “So, why did they do so many tests? Was one not enough?”

Rose tapped her notes. “The U.S. wanted to test different bomb designs, effects at various altitudes, and learn how to survive nuclear war.”

A countdown began booming over loudspeakers.

“Here comes the Sedan shot,” Lilly said. “It was a massive underground blast designed to test ‘peaceful nuclear explosions’, basically using nukes for big earth-moving jobs.”

The ground shook violently. Hayden grabbed a rock for balance.

Seconds later, a gigantic crater formed, ejecting millions of tons of dirt and rock skyward, a geyser of radioactive dust.

“That’s one of the biggest man-made craters on Earth,” Rose said. “It blew out over 12 million tons of soil. Over 320 feet deep and more than 1,200 feet wide.”

Hayden coughed as dust drifted past. “That’s some serious landscaping.”

Lilly nodded grimly. “The scientists wore protective gear, but many military personnel were dangerously close to the blasts.”

Hayden pointed to a group of soldiers lined up on a ridge, waving and saluting as the blast went off.

Rose winced. “Yep. Some were told to ‘watch the show’ from just a few miles away.”

“Seriously? That sounds insane,” Hayden said.

“It was,” Lilly agreed. “Some soldiers even performed drills in the fallout zone after the blasts to see how radiation affected them.”

Hayden’s eyes grew wide. “So people got irradiated on purpose?”

“Unfortunately, yes,” Rose said. “They were testing human limits, but with little understanding of the long-term effects.”

Suddenly, the scene shifted. The teens found themselves looking up at a pale blue sky, then downward at a group of soldiers standing in a shallow pit in the desert, their helmets shining under the sun.

Lilly explained, “This is the ‘Genie Missile’ test. One of the most controversial.”

“They made five soldiers stand directly beneath the blast,” Rose said quietly. “About a thousand feet below.”

Hayden’s mouth dropped open. “Wait, beneath a nuclear explosion? Why?”

Rose shook her head. “They wanted to see if civilians on the ground could survive a nuclear bomb that was put on a missile and shot at a formation of Soviet bombers.”

The countdown began.

“Ten… nine… eight…”

The soldiers stood there looking up, standing tall.

“Three… two… one…”

A blinding flash erupted overhead. The earth shook violently.

A deafening roar filled the air as intense heat and pressure slammed downward.

The teens felt the ground tremble beneath their feet.

When the dust settled, the soldiers stood there, dazed but alive.

Lilly narrated, “They even got a camera guy to document the whole thing.”

Hayden looked horrified. “That’s insane. They risked all of them like lab rats.”

Rose nodded. “It was a cruel reminder of how little was understood and how far the military was willing to go in the name of research.”

The teens were suddenly whisked to a scene with clouds of black smoke swirling as radioactive material spread into the air.

“This is one of the ‘dirty bomb’ tests,” Lilly said, grimacing. “They mixed nuclear blasts with conventional explosives to spread radioactive fallout.”

A scientist nearby jotted notes on radiation levels.

“Crazy part?” Rose added. “They even released radioactive animals, like pigs and monkeys, to study radiation sickness.”

Hayden gagged. “That’s… horrifying.”

Suddenly, a new blast shook the desert.

“This one’s called ‘John,’” Rose said. “It was an airburst that tested how soldiers could survive in a nuclear battlefield.”

The teens saw soldiers climbing out of trenches as the bomb exploded hundreds of meters away.

“They called it ‘atomic maneuvers,’” Lilly explained. “Troops marched toward the blast to test protective gear and tactics.”

Hayden muttered, “I’d be running the other way.”

The scene shifted to soldiers digging trenches, standing on hills, and running drills among plumes of smoke.

"This was Desert Rock," Rose said. "Military exercises designed to get troops used to fighting near nuclear blasts."

Lilly nodded. "Thousands of troops participated, often exposed to dangerous radiation."

Hayden shook his head. "This sounds more like a horror movie than a history report."

As the teens caught their breath after the "Priscilla" test, Rose pointed toward a fenced-off area with a puzzled look.

"Wait, you've gotta hear about this," she said, eyes wide. "During Operation Plumbob, there was an accident that literally launched a manhole cover into the sky."

Hayden blinked. "A manhole cover? Like, the metal cover from a sewer?"

"Exactly," Lilly said, nodding eagerly. "It was part of a test called 'Pascal-B.' Scientists placed a steel plate over a test shaft that went about 100 feet underground."

Rose continued, "When the nuclear blast went off underground, the blast pressure went up through the test shaft to the steel plate and rocketed it like a giant bullet straight up into the sky."

Hayden's jaw dropped. "So what happened to the manhole cover?"

"Well, it wasn't just any manhole cover," Rose said, "it was launched at over 125,000 miles per hour faster than Earth's escape velocity."

Lilly added, "That means it could have escaped Earth's gravity and flown into space."

Hayden looked around the Nevada desert, half-expecting to see a giant steel lid floating in the sky.

Hayden stood proud. “Since it launched at escape velocity, does that mean it was the first man-made item in space?”

Lilly chuckled. “The official reports say it probably vaporized exiting Earth’s atmosphere but there’s no way to be sure. If it did, it would have been the first man made object in space beating the USSRs satellite ‘Sputnik by almost two months.”

Hayden shook his head. “Only the Cold War would come up with a nuclear-powered manhole cover cannon.”

In Las Vegas, a large group of civilians stood on the roofs of casinos watching a mushroom cloud from miles away.

“People downwind from the tests got sick,” Lilly said. “Radiation drifted for hundreds of miles, causing health problems and birth defects.”

Hayden looked toward the horizon, sad. “So all this testing had huge human costs.”

“Exactly,” Rose said. “Operation Plumbob showed the destructive power of nuclear weapons, but at a big price.”

ALISSA suddenly spoke from the chronojumper, “We have to go the radiation levels are too high. Any longer exposure and it will be dangerous to your health. Opening a portal now.

A portal opened as the teen rushed through back to the garage.

The chronojumper powered down as the three teens sat in stunned silence.

Hayden finally broke the quiet. “I mean, it was wild… but also scary how reckless it all was.”

Lilly nodded. “It’s important to remember history, the good, the bad, and the dangerous.”

Rose smiled. “And that’s why we need to tell these stories. To learn from them.”

Hayden grinned. "Next report, maybe something less explosive?"

Rose laughed. "Or maybe more like the story of the Bikini Atoll tests."

Lilly tapped her pen. "Or the time Kodak discovered nuclear radiation spreading across America."

Hayden groaned playfully. "Just promise me no radioactive cockroaches."

They all laughed as the chronojumper was humming to life for their next adventure.

Standing Tall Against Slavery

"Okay, last one before we submit the report," Rose said, brushing the dust off the chronojumper's crystal interface. She looked determined, as always. "This time, we're going to 1800s Kentucky."

Hayden raised a hand. "Uh, does this one have dinosaurs?"

"No," Lilly said, already flipping through her notebook. "It has something better. Cassius Marcellus Clay."

Hayden squinted. "Muhammad Ali?"

Lilly beamed. "Nope. The original Cassius Clay. A politician. An abolitionist. A guy who fought slavery with words and fists. The man once brought a Bowie knife to a debate."

Hayden blinked. "That's… weirdly awesome."

"ALISSA, take us to Lexington, Kentucky. 1845." Rose commanded "Opening now."

A portal opened in the garage

"Watch, take notes, try not to get stabbed." Rose joked

"Comforting," Hayden said as the time field activated.

The teens walked through the portal and into a field near a large estate with white columns, iron fences, and American flags flapping in the breeze. The year was 1845.

"Welcome to White Hall," Lilly said. "Home of Kentucky's wildest abolitionist."

They watched from behind a hedge as a tall man in a dark waistcoat gave orders to workers installing…

"Wait," Hayden whispered. "Is that a cannon on his lawn?"

"Yep," Rose said, squinting. "Real ones. He used them to defend his anti-slavery newspaper."

They crept closer.

Clay turned, frowning. "You there, children. What business do you have sneaking around my house?"

Rose stepped forward cautiously. "We're, uh… students. Studying history. You're… kind of a legend, sir."

Clay's brow relaxed slightly. "Legend? Hardly. I just happen to believe slavery is an abomination. That shouldn't make me famous. That should make me normal."

Lilly beamed. "You started The True American, right? That paper made slave owners furious."

Clay chuckled. "They tried to silence me. Broke into my office and destroyed my press. I moved it back in and bolted the doors."

Hayden grinned. "And the cannons?"

"Loaded at all times," Clay said, stone-faced. "And when that didn't work, they tried to kill me. One man came at me with a revolver. I took seven bullets. Stabbed him with my Bowie knife."

Hayden's jaw dropped. "You got SHOT SEVEN TIMES and still won the fight?!"

"I had to crawl home," Clay said casually. "But I lived. Barely. I finished the next edition of the paper in bed."

Rose scribbled in her journal. "This is insane. Why aren't more people talking about you?"

"Because I was on the right side of history too early," Clay said. "And because most people are afraid to stand up unless someone else stands first."

They followed Clay as he showed them around the estate. He talked as he walked, his deep voice full of conviction.

"I was born into wealth," Clay said. "My father was one of the largest slaveholders in Kentucky. I grew up surrounded by slavery, but it never sat right with me. I saw what it did to people, the cruelty, the degradation, and what it did to the hearts of those who justified it."

He paused, letting them catch up. "When I came of age, I inherited land and slaves. I freed them all. That was just the beginning. I knew words had power, and I intended to use mine."

"In 1834 I was giving a speech in Kentucky where I pulled out a Bible and said 'For those of you that believe in the laws of God I present to you this argument against slavery,' I then pulled out a copy of the Constitution and said, 'For those of you that believe in the laws of man I present to you this argument against slavery,' I finally pulled out my two pistols and told the crowd 'For those of you that don't believe in the laws of God or man I give you this argument against slavery,' That's when an assassin from Louisiana came up to me and shot me in the chest"

"How are you still alive?" Rose said, confused.

"I had my trusty Bowie knife in my coat pocket. The metal stopped the bullet." Clay replied

Lilly looked at Clay, shocked when she said, "What happened next?"

Clay grinned, “I pulled that knife out and stabbed that coward until his friends came up and dragged him away.”

“Just for the record, I’m against slavery,” Hayden said with his voice trembling.

Clay laughed, “Don’t worry, I won’t hurt you. I’m not a monster; I just fight for what’s right.”

He pointed to the distant barn, where more cannons had been hidden behind bales of hay. “I published anti-slavery articles in Kentucky, where it was unpopular and dangerous. I served in the Kentucky legislature, then as a diplomat under President Abraham Lincoln.”

“You worked with Lincoln?” Rose asked, wide-eyed.

“He offered me a cabinet position,” Clay said. “Secretary of War. I turned it down and demanded he free the slaves first. Lincoln didn’t forget that. Later, he made me an ambassador to Russia. It was during my time there that I helped negotiate the deal for Alaska.”

Hayden’s mouth dropped open. “You helped buy Alaska?!”

Clay nodded. Secured the support we needed from the Tsar. I knew the geography, the politics, and the personalities.”

Rose chimed in, “That land turned out to be one of the greatest purchases in U.S. history. Gold, oil, strategic location, it has it all.”

They stopped near a stack of lumber, where workers paused to tip their hats to Clay.

“Weren’t you also in the military?” Lilly asked.

Clay gave a tight smile. “I was a captain in the Mexican-American War. Led men into battle. I’ve seen the cost of war, and I never glorify it. But sometimes, fighting is necessary. I believe in peace, but not passivity.”

"While at war, my men and I were captured by the Mexican government and held as prisoners of war. A few of my men escaped one night, and the Mexican army wanted to kill all of us as punishment. I offered my own life as I took responsibility for their actions."

"How are you still here then?" Hayden questioned.

"The Mexicans respected my honor, so they spared the lives of me and my men. They let all of us go once the war had ended."

He showed them a framed copy of his newspaper's first edition. "When I wrote the first editorial in The True American, I said, 'I am not afraid.' That wasn't just a slogan. It was my reality. People came with threats, then fists, then guns. I gave them none of my fear."

The teens stood in silence for a moment.

They heard shouting from the nearby town. A group of angry men were gathering with torches.

Clay glanced at them. "You might want to leave soon."

"But you're staying?" Hayden asked.

"I always do," Clay said. "I won't be intimidated by bullies with fire. They're afraid. That's why they shout."

He folded his arms. "They call me violent. But I use violence only to protect what matters: freedom, truth, and justice. I speak out when others whisper. That's dangerous to cowards."

Lilly nodded slowly. "You're one of the bravest people we've met."

"I'm one of the angriest," Clay corrected. "Anger can be good. If it leads to action."

He paused, then added, "You don't need to be loud to be right. But sometimes being loud is necessary. Don't let the world silence your conscience. Now go on and get out of here now. Kids should not see what is about to happen to these guys”

The chronojumper buzzed on Rose’s wrist.

“Time is up.” ALISSA said. “Opening a portal home.”

They walked through the portal and back into the garage.

Back in Rose’s garage, Hayden collapsed into the beanbag.

“THAT. GUY. WAS. NUTS.”

“Brilliant,” Lilly corrected. “And absolutely fearless.”

Rose opened her laptop. “We have our final story. ‘Cassius Clay: The Abolitionist Who Took Seven Bullets and Kept Typing.’”

Hayden leaned back. “I’m giving him a movie in my head. It’s rated R for Revolutionary.”

Lilly laughed. “History’s better with time travel.”

“And with great men willing to change the world.” Rose added.

Presenting History

Rose, Lilly and Hayden had an incredible journey, one that had carried them through some of America's strangest, most intense moments in history. They had witnessed armored bulldozers tearing through towns, a brave horse carrying wounded soldiers to safety, planes flying endless missions to save a city under siege, and even nuclear tests that pushed human limits.

Lilly exhaled, her eyes wide. "I'm still trying to wrap my head around all of it. How real it all was. These weren't just stories; these were people's lives."

Hayden slumped onto an old couch, running a hand through his hair. "And some of the stuff we saw? Totally crazy. A bulldozer turned into a tank? A duck as a war hero? I never thought history would be this… wild."

Rose smiled, but her voice carried a thoughtful edge. "It's easy to think of history as boring facts and dates. But it's the people behind those facts who make it alive. Their fears Their hopes. Their fights."

Hayden nodded slowly. "Like those veterans in Athens, standing up to corrupt cops. That was gutsy. And the soldiers under that nuclear blast? I can't even imagine."

Lilly's face grew serious. "And the Berlin Airlift. Imagine being one of those pilots, flying non-stop to keep an entire city alive during a blockade. It wasn't just about planes or politics. It was about hope."

Rose stood, flipping open her notebook. "Mr. Pellicano said this report counts for half our grade. But I don't want to just write about what happened. I want to tell the stories that show the weird, the wild, and the human side."

Hayden grinned, surprising even himself. "I'm in. Let's show everyone history isn't just old stuff in books. It's messy, crazy, and full of people like us. They didn't exactly know what they were doing but they made it work and changed history."

Lilly pulled up their photos and notes on her tablet. "We've got everything from Marvin Heemeyer's armored bulldozer to Sergeant Reckless carrying wounded soldiers, the Berlin Airlift's nonstop flights, and even the Eggnog Riot at West Point."

Rose nodded firmly. "These stories aren't just history lessons. They show people fighting for justice, for survival, and sometimes just trying to be heard."

They sat together, organizing their notes and memories, turning incredible adventures into one unforgettable project. The only problem was to figure out which story to present. They agreed to their five favorites: Grand Theft U-Boat, One Switch from Oblivion, Operation Devil Duck, The Destroyer That Couldn't Catch a Break, and The Skydiving Beavers of 1948.

"Let's do this democratically." Rose said taking lead on the decision, "We will rank the finalists by giving your favorite five points, second favorite four points and so on. Now everyone grab a paper and no looking at each others paper."

Rose, Lilly, and Hayden went to opposite sides of the garage to write. When they returned to the table the results were as follows: Grand Theft U-Boat – 7, One Switch from Oblivion –

14, Operation Devil Duck – 9, The Destroyer That Couldn't Catch a Break – 9, and The Skydiving Beavers of 1948. – 6.

"Looks like the US government nuking North Carolina wins." Rose said "Now to get this presentation ready for tomorrow."

The Next Day — Presentation Day

The classroom buzzed with chatter as Mr. Pellicano called their names.

Rose stepped forward confidently,

Rose stepped up to the front of the classroom with Lilly and Hayden close behind. She adjusted the pages in front of her and took a breath.

"Today," she began, "we're reporting on an event that nearly erased an entire state from the map. Twice. And it wasn't a war or a natural disaster. It was a mistake. A really, really close one."

Hayden nodded dramatically. "Like, nuke-the-East-Coast close."

Lilly opened her notebook. "It happened in 1961, outside Goldsboro, North Carolina. A U.S. Air Force B-52 Stratofortress was flying a Cold War mission with two live thermonuclear bombs onboard."

Rose clicked to the next slide: a blurry black-and-white photo of a B-52. "This mission was part of Operation Chrome Dome, where armed bombers flew around the clock so we could retaliate if the Soviets ever launched a nuclear attack."

Hayden pointed to the plane. "Except this one had a fuel leak. The right wing snapped off midair. The plane broke apart, and the nukes fell out."

The next slide showed a crater in a North Carolina field. Lilly spoke again: "One of the bombs deployed its parachute. The other one slammed into the ground. That one was armed and went through almost the entire detonation process."

Rose held up a drawing of the Mark 39 bomb. "It had five safety switches. Four failed. Only one stopped it from going off. One. Switch."

Hayden spread his hands. "That bomb had a yield of four megatons. It would've destroyed everything from Goldsboro to Washington D.C."

Lilly added, "And the second bomb sank deep into the mud. They never recovered all of it. Part of the core is still buried there!"

Rose continued, "We even talked to an eyewitness, an old farmer who lived nearby. He remembered the bang. He said the government told them to stay away and didn't explain much. A few cows died, and later, some neighbors got sick."

Hayden said, "One of the military guys there even said that if the plane had crashed slightly differently, if there had been just one more jolt, the bomb would've detonated."

Lilly turned a page in her notes. "After this incident, which is called a 'Broken Arrow' event, engineers completely changed the way we build and transport nukes. The safety protocols got way stricter."

Rose finished the report: "This wasn't the only accident either. There were dozens more during the Cold War. But this one came terrifyingly close to catastrophe."

Hayden said, "So yeah. We almost nuked ourselves. Twice. By accident."

Lilly closed her notebook. "We titled our report: 'One Switch from Oblivion.' Because that's what it was."

Rose stepped back as the class sat in stunned silence.

Then Hayden grinned. "Next time, we're doing something fun. Maybe a goat that flew a plane."

A few students laughed nervously.

When they finished, Mr. Pellicano smiled broadly. “You didn’t just tell history, you brought it alive. These stories remind us that history is made by real people, with real fears and real courage. I do want to clear something up real quick. Did you say you talked to an eyewitness?”

Rose got very nervous, “Yeah, Um, I meant we read eyewitness reports.”

“Good save.” Hayden whispered.

"Class, look at this report," Mr. Pellicano said from the front of the room. "It perfectly captures the real value of history. We find these important lessons tucked away in the past, like how our fear of the Soviet Union drove us to take terrifying risks. In this instance, we quite literally dodged two nuclear strikes. But before you head out, remember this: the best part of studying history is that if you look closely enough, you can actually predict the future."

After class, the school emptied around them as the three friends walked out, a calm settling over the afternoon.

Lilly said softly, “I used to think history was just stuff that happened long ago. But it’s really about why people did what they did and how it still shapes our world.”

Hayden laughed. “And who knew a ‘D’ student like me could learn so much?”

Rose smiled warmly at them both. “We’re not just students. We’re witnesses. And maybe, just maybe, next time we’ll find a story even stranger… and maybe even change history ourselves.”

They glanced back toward the garage where the chronojumper waited, its quiet hum promising new adventures.

Because history isn’t just behind us.

It’s alive. Waiting to be discovered.

Acknowledgments

The author would like to personally thank:

Rose, Lilly, & Hayden – For inspiring me to write this book and being the inspiration for the characters.

Alissa Depietro – For being my Editor, Best friend, and Biggest critic.

Christopher Pellicano Sr (Dad), Mary Jo Adamita (Mom), Lisa Pellicano (Stepmom), Salvatore Adamita (Stepdad) – For raising me right.

My Siblings Christopher Pellicano Jr, Dominic Adamita, Salvatore Adamita Jr, Joseph Adamita, Samule Adamita, Mary Adamita, & Jessica Pellicano – For always being there for me.

Nic "The Fat Electrician", Brandon Herrera, and the rest of the Unsubscribe crew – For reigniting my love of history.

All my history teachers – For teaching me history can be fun.

Everybody who supported my first book "Surviving Vegas" – For taking a chance on an unknown author from nowhere Florida.

About the Author

Ant Pellicano is a first-time children's author with a passion for storytelling, history, and adventure. After years of working in security and witnessing human nature up close, he turned his attention to inspiring the next generation through books that make learning fun and unforgettable.

Drawing on his lifelong love of American history and his vivid imagination, Ant created a series that follows three curious kids as they travel through time, landing in the middle of the country's most unexpected and often overlooked moments. His writing blends humor, heart, and just enough chaos to keep young readers turning the pages.

When he's not writing, Ant enjoys spending time with his family, friends, and hanging out with his tortoise, Bowser. If you'd like to know more, you can follow him on X/Twitter @antpellicano.

www.ingramcontent.com/pod-product-compliance
Ingram Content Group UK Ltd.
Pitfield, Milton Keynes, MK11 3LW, UK
UKHW022023190726
13853UKWH00005B/2081